ARCTIC TRANSFORMATIONS

Carvers at Fenbrook

ARCTIC TRANSFORMATIONS

Carvers at Fenbrook

Seraphim Editions

IN CO-OPERATION WITH

Correctional Service of Canada

The publisher gratefully acknowledges the financial assistance of the Canada Council for the Arts.

Canada Council for the Arts | Conseil des Arts du Canada

Published in 2004 by
Seraphim Editions
238 Emerald Street North
Hamilton, Ontario
Canada L8L 5K8

www.seraphimeditions.com

NATIONAL LIBRARY OF CANADA CATALOGUING IN PUBLICATION

Arctic transformations : carvers at Fenbrook / editor, Allan Briesmaster.

Translation into Inuktitut by Myna Ishulutak.
Text in English and Inuktitut.
ISBN 0-9689723-9-X

1. Inuit artists – Canada – Biography. 2. Inuit sculpture – Canada – Pictorial works. 3. Inuit prisoners – Ontario – Gravenhurst. 4. Fenbrook Institution. I. Ishulutak, Myna II. Briesmaster, Allan

E99.E7A727 2004 730'.89'9712071 C2003-907347-5

EDITOR: Allan Briesmaster
TRANSLATOR: Myna Ishulutak
DESIGNER: Carleton Wilson
ARTIST PORTRAITS: Janice Marin
ART PHOTOS: Waddington's Auctioneers & Appraisers, Toronto
COVER PHOTOS: Janice Marin and Waddington's Auctioneers & Appraisers
MAP: Courtesy of Feheley Fine Arts by Epiculture Inc., www.epiculture.com

PRINTED AND BOUND IN CANADA

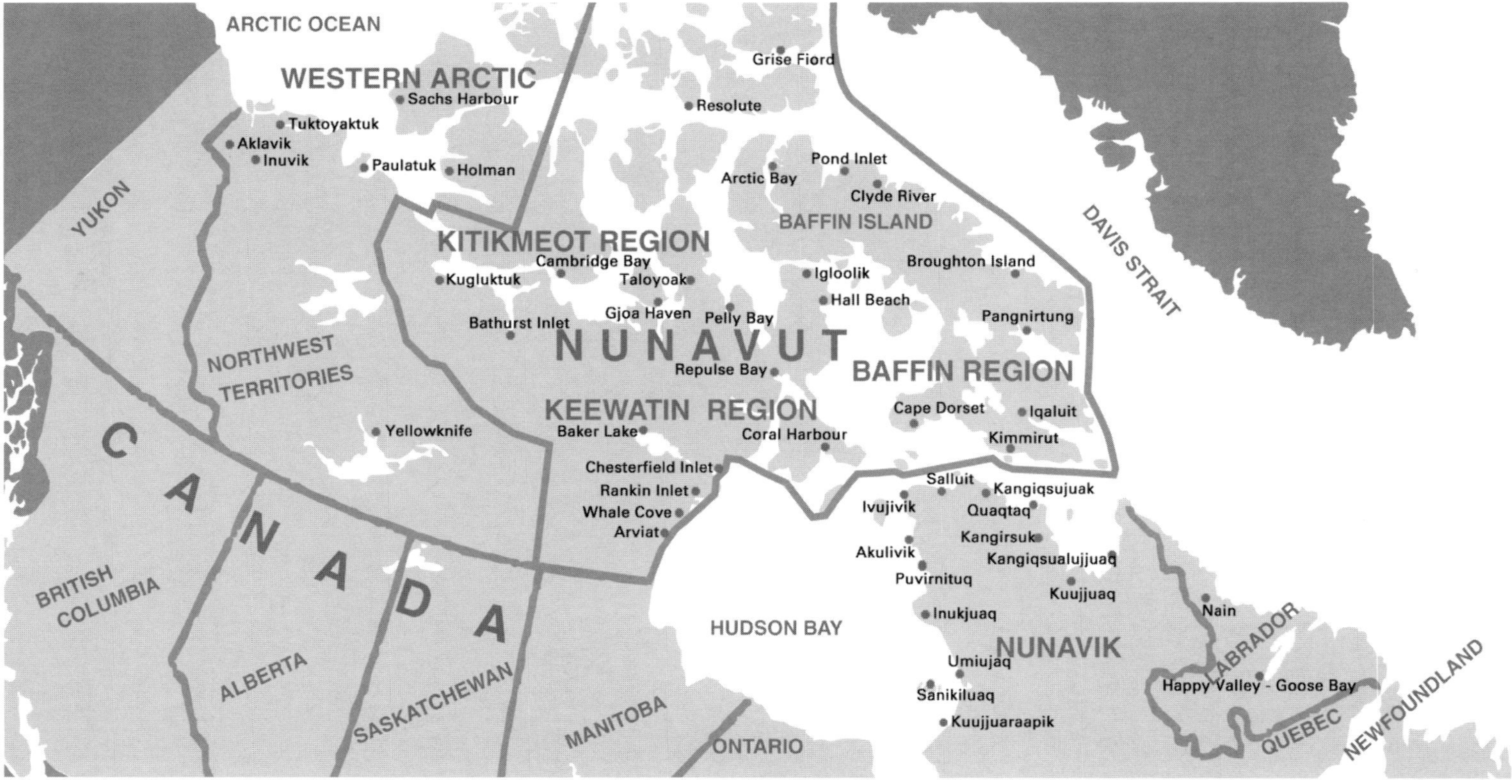
ARCTIC OCEAN
WESTERN ARCTIC
Sachs Harbour
Tuktoyaktuk
Aklavik
Inuvik
Paulatuk
Holman
YUKON
Grise Fiord
Resolute
Pond Inlet
Arctic Bay
Clyde River
BAFFIN ISLAND
DAVIS STRAIT
KITIKMEOT REGION
Cambridge Bay
Kugluktuk
Taloyoak
Gjoa Haven
Pelly Bay
Bathurst Inlet
Igloolik
Hall Beach
Broughton Island
Pangnirtung
NUNAVUT
Repulse Bay
BAFFIN REGION
NORTHWEST TERRITORIES
KEEWATIN REGION
Baker Lake
Coral Harbour
Cape Dorset
Iqaluit
Kimmirut
Yellowknife
Chesterfield Inlet
Rankin Inlet
Whale Cove
Arviat
Salluit
Kangiqsujuak
Ivujivik
Quaqtaq
Kangirsuk
Akulivik
Kangiqsualujjuaq
Puvirnituq
Kuujjuaq
CANADA
BRITISH COLUMBIA
ALBERTA
SASKATCHEWAN
MANITOBA
ONTARIO
HUDSON BAY
Inukjuaq
Nain
NUNAVIK
LABRADOR
Umiujaq
Happy Valley - Goose Bay
Sanikiluaq
Kuujjuaraapik
QUEBEC
NEWFOUNDLAND

CONTENTS

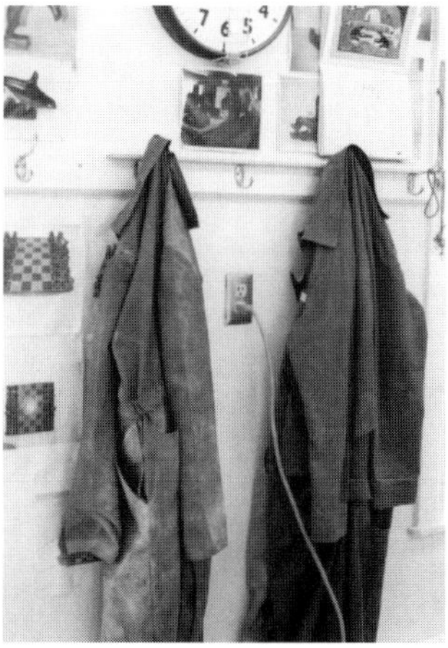

ᖃᓄᕐᑐᕋᓪᓗᓂ ᖃᓄᑐᐃᓐᓇᖅ ᓴᖅᑭᔪᖕᒍᓂᖕᒋᓐᓂᒃ ᑕᑯᓴᕈᓪᓗᑎᓪᓗ. ᐅᓇ ᐱᓗᐊᖅᑐᒥᒃ.

ᐊᕐᕋᒍᑲᓪᓚᐅᓕᖅᑐᓂᒃ, ᐅᖃᓕᒫᒐᓕᐅᖅᑎᐅᔪᖅ, ᒪᓇᓐ ᐅᕙᐃᑦ, ᐃᔅᓯᕙᓚᐅᖅᓯᒪᒻᒪᑦ ᐅᕙᖓ ᐊᓪᓚᕕᖓᓂ ᐅᖃᐅᑎᓪᓗᒍ ᐅᖃᓕᒫᒐᐅᔪᒥᒃ ᓴᖅᑭᑎᑎᒍᒪᓂᕋᑦᑐᖓ, ᐊᑎᓕᒻᒥᒃ ᑕᕐᓂᕋ ᓯᐊᖅᑲᔪᖅ, ᑖᓐᓇ ᐃᑦᑕᕐᓂᑐᖃᓐᓂᒃ ᑲᒪᔾᔭᐅᓪᓗᓂ, ᐊᖅᑯᑎᐅᓪᓗᑎᒃ ᐃᓄᓐᐃᑦ ᑎᒍᔭᐅᖅᑲᔪᑦ. ᑕᐃᔅᓱᒪᓂ ᐱᕆᐊᖅᑎᑎᕙᓪᓕᐊᓕᑕᐃᓐᓇᓚᐅᓯᒪᒐᒪ ᐊᑭᓕᖅᓱᑕᐅᖕᒋᓪᓗᓂ ᑭᓇᐅᔭᑯᑦ ᓴᖅᑭᑎᑎᒐᓱᓂᕐᒥᒃ. ᐱᔾᔪᑎᒋᓪᓗᒍ ᓴᖅᑭᑕᐅᕐᑯᓪᓗᒋᑦ ᓴᓇᖑᐊᒐᐃᑦ ᐃᓄᓐᓄᑦ ᑎᒍᔭᐅᓯᒪᕕᒻᒦᑐᑦ ᓴᓇᖑᐊᖅᑕᒥᓂᑦ ᐊᓐᑎᐅᓇᔪᒥ, ᑐᕋᓐᑐᒥᒃ ᑭᓇᐅᔭᓂᒃ ᓄᐊᓴᐃᓂᒃᑯᑦ ᐊᑭᑦᑐᕋᓐᓂᖅᒥᒃ ᑐᓂᓯᕐᑯᓪᓗᒋᑦ ᐊᖏᕋᒥᓄᑦ ᓄᓇᕗᒻᒥ. ᐅᖃᐅᓯᓇᓪᓗᒍ ᑕᒪᓐᓇ ᑕᐃᒪᐃᒍᒪᓂᕋ ᒪᓇᓐᒧ, ᖁᕕᐊᓚᐅᖅᑐᖅ ᐊᔅᓱᐊᓗᒃ, ᐅᖅᑦᑐᓂᓗ ᐊᔅᓱᐊᓗᒃ ᐱᐅᒐᔪᖅᑐᖅ ᐅᖃᓕᒪᒐᐊᓇᓗᒍ.

ᐃᓱᒪᒋᔭᕗᑦ ᑕᒪᑭᖅᑐᓄᒃ ᐅᖃᐅᓯᕆᓂᕋᑦᑎᒍ ᓴᓇᖑᐊᖅᑎᓄᑦ. ᐊᖏᖃᑎᒋᑦᑐᐃᓐᓇᐅᓚᐅᖅᑐᐃᑦ ᓴᓇᖑᐊᖅᑎᑦ ᑕᓱᒥᖓ ᐃᓱᒪᒋᔭᑦᑎᓐᓂᒃ ᐊᒻᒪᓗ ᐅᐊᑎᐊᕈᓂᓴᒥᖓᓯᒪᓪᓗᓂ... ᑭᓯᐊᓂ ᐱᔭᕐᓂᖏᑦᑐᖅ ᐅᐊᑎᑦᐊᕈᓐᓂᓴᐅᑎᓪᓗᒍ. ᑖᓐᓇ ᐊᑭᑐᑦᕋᓐᓂᖅ ᓴᓇᖑᐊᒐᓐᓂᒃ ᐅᖅᑲᓕᒪᒻᒥ ᐅᖅᓯᒪᓪᓗᓂ, ᐊᒻᒪᓗ ᓇᒻᒥᓂᖅ ᐃᓅᓯᕐᒥᓂᒃ ᐅᖅᑲᐅᓯᖅᑲᑦᑐᑎᒃ ᐊᒻᒪᓗ ᐊᔾᔨᓕᐅᓯᒪᔪᑦ ᐅᖃᓕᒪᒻᒥᑐ, ᑭᓯᐊᓂ ᐊᓯᑎᕆᓗᒍ ᑲᔪᔾᔪᓐᓇᖅᑲᑦ ᐊᒥᓱᑦ ᐃᓄᐃᑦ ᐊᔪᕆᓐᓂᖅᑭᑦ ᑕᑯᔭᐅᕐᑯᓪᓗᑎᑦ.

ᑎᒍᔭᐅᓯᒪᕕᒃ ᐃᓂᕆᓪᓗᒍ ᐱᔭᓇᐊᖃᖕᒋᒻᒪᑦ ᖃᓄᕐᑐᓂᕐᒥᒃ. ᑎᒍᔭᐅᓯᒪᕕᓪᓗ ᐃᓱᒪᖅᓱᓇᖕᒋᒻᒪᑦ ᑕᐃᒫᓪᓗ ᒪᓕᒐᐅᒻᒪᑦ ᑭᓯᐊᓂᓕ ᓴᖅᑭᑎᑦᑎᕙᓪᓕᐊᕐᑯᓪᓗᒋᑦ ᐱᐅᔪᒥᒃ ᓄᓇᒥᓐᓄᑦ ᐅᑎᖅᑎᑎᓗᑎᒃ. ᑕᑯᐊ 9_ᖑᔪᑦ ᓴᓇᖑᐊᖅᑏᑦ ᑎᒍᔭᐅᖅᑲᔪᑦ ᐅᐱᕆᔭᐅᓪᓗᑎᒃ ᐃᓚᒍᒪᓂᖏᑦ ᐊᒻᒪᓗ ᓱᒍᓐᓇᓂᖏᑦ ᖃᓄᐃᑦᑐᒥᓐᓂᖏᓐᓂᒃ ᑎᒍᔭᐅᓯᒪᕕᒻᒥ ᑕᐸᓇᖏᑦᑐᒥᒃ ᐅᖓᓯᑦᑑᓪᓗᓂᓗ ᐊᖏᕋᒥᒃ, ᑖᒃᑯᐊ ᐱᕈᑎᑎᓚᐅᖅᑐᑦ ᐱᐅᔫᑎᓂᒃ ᓴᓇᖑᐊᒐᒃᑯᑦ ᐅᖓᑕᓄᑦ 14,000 ᑐᓂᓯᓪᓗᑎᒃ ᐃᓪᓕᑏᑦ ᑲᑐᔾᔮᖃᑎᕇᖕᒋᓐᓄᑦ ᓄᓇᕗᒥ.

ᑕᓐᓇ ᑲᒪᒋᓪᓗᒍ ᐊᒥᓱᓂᒃ ᐱᔭᓯᖃᓐᓇᖓᑦ, ᖄᖓᒍᒃᑲᓐᓂᖅ ᐱᑕᓇᑎᑦᑎᓇᖓᑦ, ᐊᒥᓱᓪᓗ ᐃᖅᑲᓇᐃᔭᖅᑏᑦ ᑎᒍᔭᐅᓯᒪᕕᒻᒥ, ᐅᑯᐊ ᐊᑎᖏᑦ ᓚᑎᐊ ᑯᐊᓪᓴᒃ, ᐃᓄᐃᑦ ᑲᒪᔩᖓᑦ, ᔩᒻ ᓯᐸᐃᓱ ᐃᓄᐃᑦ ᑐᑭᒧᐊᑎᑎᔩᖓᑦ, ᐊᒻᒪᓗ ᐱᓗᐊᖅᑐᒥᒃ ᓯᐅᕕᐊ ᐳᐊᑕᓐ ᓇᒥᓂᖃᑦᑎᐅᔪᖅ ᑐᑭᒧᐊᑎᑎᔩᐅᓪᓗᓂ ᑕᒪᒃᑯᓗᖓ, ᑖᓐᓇ

FOREWORD

Perhaps all creative works are the result of a serendipitous array of factors. This one certainly was.

A year ago, the publisher of Seraphim Editions, Maureen Whyte, sat in my office promoting the launch of another book, *My Spirit Wonders*, an anthology of art, prose and poetry produced by people in prison. At that time, I was just in the beginning stages of developing an interesting art-for-charity initiative. The idea was to use art produced by Inuit Carvers housed in a federal prison in Ontario, and sell it by auction in Toronto to raise money for a charity in the Carvers' home territory of Nunavut. As I described this project to Maureen, she exclaimed, "that would make a wonderful book!"

Together we took the idea of the book to the Carvers group. They agreed to the idea and the rest is history . . . but not quite that easy a history. The charity art auction on which this book is based, and the collection of autobiographies and photographs for this book, required the hard work and persistence and creativity of many people.

Prison is not an easy place to be creative! The impact of an institution designed to restrict liberties can severely impair the ability to create and the desire to freely contribute back to the community. These nine artists must be commended for their willingness and ability to rise above the effects of being in prison in a strange land far away from home, to produce wonderful art that raised over $14,000 for the Illitiit Society in Nunavut.

The project's success is also a result of the extra work, beyond the call of duty, by several staff at Fenbrook Institution, including Leetia Kowalchuk, the Inuit Liaison; Jim Spicer, Inuit programs coordinator; and especially Sylvia Purdon, Private Sector Liaison, who coordinated the project from the institution side. Sylvia even came into the institution on weekends and holidays so the carving shed could be open extra hours for the fellows working so hard to complete the items for auction. The

ᑐᑭᒧᐊᑎᑎᔪᓐᓇᓚᐅᖓᑦ ᑖᔅᓱᒥᖓ ᑭᒐᑐᖅᑐᒍ ᑎᒍᔭᐅᓯᒪᕕᒃ. ᐊᓪᓛᓗᓐᓃᑦ ᓯᐅᕕᐊ ᑎᒍᔭᐅᓯᒪᕕᒻᒧᖃᑦᑕᒪᕆᓚᐅᖅᑐᖅ ᐱᓇᓱᐊᕈᓯᐅᑉ ᓄᖑᐊᓂ ᐊᒻᒪᓗ ᕿᑲᓐᓇᐅᒐᓗᐊᒃᑯᑦ ᓴᓇᖑᐊᖅᕕᒃ ᒪᑐᐃᖓᖁᓪᓗᓂᐅᒃ ᐱᔭᕆᕈᓐᓇᖁᓪᓗᒋᑦ ᓴᓇᖑᐊᑏᑦ ᐊᑭᑦᑐᕋᐅᑎᐅᓂᐊᖅᑐᓂ. ᐊᒥᓱᓪᓗ ᐱᖃᑕᐅᓪᓗᑎᒃ ᐃᑲᔪᖅᓯᑕᐅᓪᓗᑎᓪᓗ ᐃᖅᑲᓇᐃᔭᖅᑎᓄᑦ ᑎᒍᔭᐅᓯᒪᕕᒻᒥ, ᐱᖃᑕᐅᓪᓗᓂᓗ ᐊᐅᓚᑎᔨᖓ ᑎᒍᔭᐅᓯᒪᕕᐅᑉ, ᐊᒻᒪᓗ ᑐᖏᓕᖓ ᐊᓯᖏᓪᓗ, ᑕᒪᓐᓇᓗ ᑲᔪᓯᑎᐊᓚᐅᖅᑐᖅ ᐸᕐᓇᑕᐅᔪᖅ.

ᐊᑭᑦᑐᕋᐅᑎᓂᖅ ᐅᕝᕙᓗ ᐅᖃᓕᒫᒐᓕᐅᖅᓂᖅ ᑲᔪᓯᓂᐊᓚᐅᖏᑦᑐᖅ ᐅᑯᐊᖑᓚᐅᖏᑉᐸᑕ: ᑭᓇᐅᔭᓴᖅᓇᑎᒃ ᐃᓪᓗᒥᒃ ᐊᑐᕐᓂᖅ ᑐᕌᓐᑐᒥ. ᐸᓪ ᐱᕼᐃᓕ ᐊᒻᒪᓗ ᐱᕼᐃᓕ ᐃᓄᐃᑦ ᓴᓇᐅᒐᐃᔭᕐᕕᖓᑦ, ᑕᒃᑭᓐ ᒪᑲᓚᐃᓐ ᐊᒻᒪᓗ ᔦᐊᑎᑕᖕ ᐊᑭᑦᑐᕋᐅᑎᑎᕐᑎᔨᖏᑦ, ᑲᑐᕆᓐ ᒥᓄᓐ ᐊᒻᒪᓗ ᑕᐃᒫᓪᓗᐊᖅ ᓴᓇᐅᒐᐃᔭᖅᑎᑦ, ᐊᑐᐃᓇᐅᑎᑦᑎᓪᓗᑎᒃ ᐱᓕᒻᒪᔅᓯᒪᔪᓂᒃ ᑲᑎᒪᔩᓂᒃ, ᐅᖃᓯᒪᔦᑦ ᑐᕋᕈᑎᖏᑦ, ᑕᑯᒥᓇᖅᓯᑎᑕᐅᓪᓗᓂ ᐊᒻᒪᓗ ᑕᒧᓗᒐᔅᓴᓂᒃ ᐊᑐᐃᓐᓇᐅᑎᑦᑎᔪᑦ, ᑐᔅᓴᐅᒪᑎᑦᑎᔮᓪᓗ, ᑐᔅᓴᐅᒪᑎᑦᑎᔮᑦ, ᐊᒻᒪᓗ ᑎᑭᔮᔅᓴᐃᑦ ᐊᒥᓱᕈᑎᑕᐅᓂᖏᑦ. ᐊᓐᑎᐅᕆᔫᒥ ᐃᓕᓐᓂᐊᕐᕕᒃ ᓴᓇᓂᖅᒧᑦ ᓴᓇᕈᓗᔭᕐᓂᖅᒧᑦ ᐊᒻᒪᓗ ᐃᓕᓐᓂᐊᖅᑎᐅᔪᖅ ᔭᓇᔅ ᒪᕆᓐ ᐃᑲᔪᓚᐅᓂᖓᓗ, ᐱᓕᕆᖃᑎᖃᑦᑎᐊᖅᑐᓂ ᑎᒍᔭᐅᓯᒪᔪᓂᒃ ᑎᑎᕋᕋᓱᑦᑎᓪᓗᒋᓪᓗ ᐃᓄᓯᖓᑕ ᒥᔅᓴᓄᑦ ᐃᑲᔪᑎᐊᓚᐅᖓᑦ, ᐊᔾᔨᓕᐅᕆᓂᒃᑯᓪᓗ, ᑕᕐᕆᔭᓴᓕᐅᕆᓪᓗᓂᓗ ᑕᒪᓐᓇ ᑲᒪᒋᔭᐅᑎᓪᓗᒍ, ᓴᓇᖑᐊᖅᑎᒧᑦ ᑐᓂᔭᐅᑲᓂᖅᑐᑎᓪᓗ ᑎᑎᖅᑐᒐᖅᒥᒃ ᐊᑭᑐᕋᐅᑎᒍᑕᐅᓂᐊᖅᑐᒥᒃ.

ᖁᔭᓕᔪᖓ ᑕᒪᓐᓇ ᑐᑭᒧᐊᒐᓱᑦᑐᒍ ᖁᕕᐊᓇᓚᐅᖓᑦ ᖃᐅᔨᓴᖅᑎᐅᑎᓪᓗᖓ ᓄᓇᓕᓐᓄᑦ ᐱᓕᕆᐊᒪ ᐃᓚᒥᒻᒪᒍ ᑎᒍᔭᐅᓯᒪᕕᒻᒥ ᑲᓇᑕᒥ ᐱᓗᐊᖅᑐᒥᒃ ᐊᓐᑎᐅᕆᔫᒥ ᐸᓕᓯᖑᐊᑦ ᑐᕋᖅᑐᒥᒃ, ᐊᔅᓯᐊᓗᒃ ᐱᕙᓪᓕᖅᑎᑕᐅᓇᓚᐅᖓᑦ.

ᐃᕙᓐ ᕼᐃᔅ
ᑐᕌᓐᑐ, ᑲᓇᑕ

support and involvement of many other staff at the institution, including the Warden, and several Assistant Wardens, was also vital for the success of the project.

Neither the auction nor the book would have been possible without one more significant component: volunteers in the Toronto arts community. Pat Feheley and Feheley Fine Arts Inuit Art Gallery, Duncan McLean and Waddington's Appraisers and Auctioneers, and Kathryn Minard and Contemporary Fine Art Services Inc. provided wise counsel, address lists, venues and refreshments for events, advertising, and catalogue printing. Ontario College of Art and Design Community Arts Program student Janice Marin assisted with relationship-building with the artists, helped the men write their autobiographies, helped with the photography, made a video of the event, and contributed a painting of one of the carvers for auction.

I had the privilege of somehow coordinating all this disparate activity in my role as Community Outreach Coordinator with the Correctional Service Canada Central District (Ontario) Parole Office in Toronto. A very rewarding endeavour indeed!

Evan Heise
Toronto

ᓴᓇᖑᐊᖅᑎᑦ ᐅᑭᐅᑕᑐᒥᖓᖅᓯᒪᔪᑦ ᑎᒍᔭᐅᓯᒪᕕᒻᒥ

ᑎᒍᔭᐅᓯᒪᕕᒃ ᑎᒃᑯᐊᑕᐅᓚᐅᖅᓯᒪᒻᒪᑦ ᐃᖅᑲᑐᐃᔨᓕᕆᔨᒃᑯᓐᓂᒃ ᑲᓇᑕᒥ ᐃᓕᓯᕕᐅᒍᓐᓇᕐᓗᓂᓗ ᐊᕐᕿᒎᑉ ᒪᕈᒃ ᐅᖓᑖᓄᑦ ᑎᒍᔭᐅᓯᒪᓂᐊᖅᑲᑕ ᓄᓇᕗᑦ ᓄᑕᖑᓕᖅᑎᓪᓗᒍ ᐅᑭᐅᖅᑕᖅᑐᒥ.

ᐊᐅᓚᑎᔨᐅᓪᓗᓂ, ᑕᑯᓯᒪᓕᖅᑕᒃᑯᑦ ᐱᕙᓕᖅᓯᒪᓂᖏᑦ ᐃᓄᐃᑦ ᑎᒍᔭᐅᓯᒪᕙᑦᑐᑦ ᓴᓇᖑᐊᓂᒃᑯᑦ ᑭᓇᐅᔭᓕᐅᓂᑯᓪᓗ. ᑯᐊᐳᕆᓴᒃᑯᓐᓄᑦ.

ᐃᓄᐃᑦ ᓴᓇᖑᐊᖅᑏᑦ ᐃᖅᑲᓇᐃᔭᕈᓐᓇᖓᑕ ᒪᓕᑉᐸᒍ ᒪᓕᒋᐊᓕᓂ ᑎᒍᔭᐅᓯᒪᓂᕐᒥᓂ ᐊᒻᒪᓗ ᐃᓄᓯᕐᒥᓂᒃ ᐱᓂᐊᓂᖃᑦᑎᐊᖁᓪᓗᒍ ᑎᒍᔭᐅᓯᒪᕕᒃᑯᑦ. ᐊᑕᖏᐸᓗᑦᑐᑎᒃ ᓴᓇᖑᐊᖅᑏᑦ ᐅᓪᓘᑉ ᐊᕙᐃᓐᓇᖓᓂ ᐊᒻᒪᓗ ᐅᓪᓘᑉ ᐊᕝᕙᖓᓂᒃ ᐃᓕᓐᓂᐊᖅᑐᑎᒃ ᑎᒍᔭᐅᓯᒪᕕᒻᒥ ᐃᓕᓐᓂᐊᕆᐊᓕᓂ ᒪᓕᓪᓗᒍ. ᑕᒃᑯᐊ ᑲᑎᑦᑐᒋᑦ ᑎᒍᔭᐅᓯᒪᔪᑦ ᐃᓄᐃᑦ 25-35 ᑭᓯᐊᓂᓕ ᓴᓇᖑᐊᐸᑦᑐᑦ 12-15ᒧᑦ ᐊᒥᓱᓂᖏᑦ.

ᓴᓇᖑᐊᐸᑦᑕᖏᑦ ᐅᒃᑯᓯᔅᓴᐃᑦ, ᓇᓗᓇᐃᓯᓪᓚᕆᐸᑦᑐᑦ ᐃᓄᐃᑦ ᓇᑭᖓᓯᒪᓂᖏᓐᓂᒃ ᐃᓕᖅᑯᓯᖅᒥᒍᑦ. ᐅᑦᑐᑎᒋᓗᒍ ᑐᑦᑐ, ᐊᐃᕕᖅ, ᕿᓚᓗᒐᖅ ᐊᒻᒪᓗ ᓇᑎᑦ, ᓇᓄᐃᑦ, ᐃᓚᔮᕆᑦ ᐅᕝᕙᓗ ᐊᖓᑯᖑᐊᑎᒍᑦ ᑕᐃᒪᒐᓚᒃ ᓴᓇᖑᐊᐸᑦᑐᑦ.

ᖃᐅᔨᓴᖅᑏᑦ ᖃᐅᔨᒃᑲᐃᓯᒪᓕᖅᒥᔪᑦ ᑎᒍᔭᐅᓯᒪᔪᑦ ᐅᑎᕋᐃᒐᒥᒃ ᓄᓇᒥᓐᓄᑦ ᐃᖅᑲᓇᐃᔮᖅᓴᑕᖃᖏᓐᓂᖓᓂ. ᓴᓇᖑᐊᑳᓗᒐᓗᐊᖅᑐᑎᒃ ᐊᒻᒪᓗ ᖃᐅᔨᒪᓕᖅᑐᑎᒃ ᓴᓇᖑᐊᕆᐊᓴᖅ, ᑎᒍᔭᐅᓯᒪᕕᒻᒥᑦᑐᑦ ᖃᓪᓗᓈᓂ ᐃᓄᐃᑦ ᓴᓇᖑᐊᖅᑎᑦ ᑭᓇᐅᔭᓕᐅᕈᑎᖃᕈᓐᓇᕐᓂᖅᓴᐅᕙᑦᑐᑦ ᐅᑎᕋᐃᒐᒥᒃ ᐃᓚᒥᓄᑦ ᓴᓇᖑᐊᒐᑎᒍᑦ.

ᓴᓇᖑᐊᖅᑎᓕᒫᑦ ᓄᐊᓴᐃᒐᓯᐊᖅᑎᓄᑦ ᑭᓇᐅᔭᓕᐅᕈᑎᐅᓚᐅᖅᑐᓂᒃ ᑐᓂᓯᓚᐅᖅᑐᑦ ᐃᓪᓕᑏᑦ ᑲᑎᒪᔨᖏᓐᓄᑦ ᓄᓇᕗᒥ, ᑖᒃᑯᐊᓗ ᐱᓕᕆᔩᑦ ᑲᒪᔨᐅᔩᖑᔪᑦ ᐱᓂᕐᓗᑕᐅᓯᒪᔪᓂᒃ ᐃᑲᔪᖅᑎᑕᐅᓪᓗᑎᒃ ᐊᒻᒪᓗ ᐊᖏᕋᖃᖏᑐᒃᑯᕕᒻᒥ.

ᑕᐃᒫᒃ ᐱᕕᔅᓴᖃᑎᑎᑎᐊᖅᑐᐃᑦ ᐅᕙᑎᓐᓂᒃ ᐊᒻᒪᓗ ᑭᖑᒪᑎᔨᓂᒃ ᓄᓇᕗᒻᒥ, ᓄᓇᒋᓪᓗᓂᐅᓪᓗ ᐃᓄᐃᑦ.

ᐃᓚᓐᓈᓯ,
ᒪᐃᒃ ᐳᕙᓐ
ᐊᐅᓚᑎᔨᐅᔪᖅ
ᑎᒍᔭᐅᓯᒪᕕᒻᒥ ᖃᓪᓗᓇᓂ
ᒍᕋᐃᕙᓐᕼᐅᔅ, ᐊᓐᑎᐅᕆᔪ

THE FENBROOK INUIT ARCTIC CARVING CO-OPERATIVE

Fenbrook Institution is designated by the Correctional Service of Canada to receive federal offenders from the new territory of Nunavut located in the Eastern Arctic.

As Warden, I have been pleased to observe the progress the Inuit offenders have made in their carving business, the Fenbrook Arctic Carving Co-operative.

The Inuit Carvers qualify for the job of Inuk Carver by following their Correctional Plan and maintaining good institutional behaviour. Most carvers are half-time carvers and participate half-day in either school or correctional programs. Out of a population of 25–35 Inuit there are usually 12–15 active carvers.

Through soapstone carving, Inuit express the deepest meanings in their culture. The caribou, the walrus, whales and seals, polar bears, family groups and the magic of the Shaman frequently find expression in the art of the Inuit.

Research has shown that employment after release is essential to successful reintegration when offenders return to their home communities. With strong carving skills and good marketing knowledge, the Fenbrook Inuit Carvers have a better chance to earn a legitimate living for themselves and their families back home.

All of the Carvers in the Charity Art Auction donated the sculptures to the cause of the Illitiit Society of Nunavut, an organization that provides direct services to victims and the homeless in Iqaluit.

This was a great opportunity for us all to contribute directly to those in need in Nunavut, the home of the Inuit.

Mike Provan, Warden
Fenbrook Institution, Gravenhurst, Ontario

ᐱᒋᐊᕈᑎᒋᓗᒋᑦ ᓴᓇᙳᐊᕐᐸᑦᑐᖅ ᑎᒍᔭᐅᓯᒪᕕᒻᒥ

ᓴᓇᙳᐊᕕᒃ ᐅᑭᐅᑕᖅᑐᒥᐅᓄᑦ ᐃᓄᐃᑦ ᑎᒍᔭᐅᓯᒪᕕᒻᒥᖕᒐ ᑯᐊᐳᓇᓴᓐ ᓴᖅᑭᑕᐅᓚᐅᖅᓯᒪᒻᒪᑦ ᑎᒍᔭᐅᓯᒪᕕᒻᒥ ᖃᓪᓗᓈᓂ ᐱᕕᓴᖅᑯᓪᓗᒋᑦ ᑎᒍᔭᐅᓯᒪᕙᑦᑐᑦ ᖃᓪᓗᓈᓂ ᓴᓇᙳᐊᕈᓐᓇᖅᑎᑕᐅᓪᓗᑎᒃ ᐅᒃᑯᓯᔅᓴᒥᒃ ᓂᐅᕈᑎᒋᔪᓐᓇᖅᓗᒍ. ᓴᓇᙳᐊᖃᑦᑕᓕᖅᑎᓪᓗᒋᑦ ᐃᓄᐃᑦ ᐱᒋᐅᑲᓂᖅᓯᒪᕗᑦ ᖃᓄᕐᓗ ᑐᑭᓯᐅᒪᑲᓐᓂᓕᕐᑐᑎᒃ ᓂᐅᕈᑎᖃᓐᓂᐅᑉ ᒥᔅᓵᓄᑦ ᐱᔭᕆᐊᑭᑦᑐᖕᒋᓐᓂᖕᒐᓂᓪᓗ.

ᐊᓂᒐᐃᒻᒪᑕ ᑎᒍᔭᐅᓯᒪᕕᒻᒥᒃ ᐊᖕᒋᕋᖅᑐᑎᒃ ᓄᓇᒥᓐᓄᑦ, ᐱᔪᓐᓇᓕᖅᑎᑎᑲᓐᓂᐸᑦᑐᑦ ᐃᓪᓗᒥᐅᖅᑲᑎᒥᓂᓪᓗ ᐃᑲᔫᑎᖃᓐᓂᓴᐅᓕᖅᑐᑎᒃ ᑭᓇᐅᔭᓕᐅᓂᒃᑯᑦ ᐃᓕᑉᐸᓕᓂᕆᔭᓂ ᐊᑐᖅᑐᓂᐅᑉ ᖃᓄᕐᓗ ᓂᐅᕈᑎᖃᓐᓂᒻᒥᒃ ᓴᓇᙳᐊᒐᓐᓂᒃ. ᐸᕐᓇᓂᖅᒥᒃ ᓯᕗᓂᔅᓴᒧᑦ ᖃᓄᕐᓗ ᐸᐸᓯᑲᓐᓂᓂᕐᒥᒃ ᑭᓇᐅᔭᓕᐅᕈᑎᓕᐅᖅᑕᒥᓂᒃ ᓴᓇᙳᐊᓂᒃᑯᑦ.

ᐊᐱᕆᔭᐅᒐᐃᒐᒥᓪᓗ ᖃᓄᐃᑦᑐᒥᒃ ᐱᔭᕆᓯᓛᕈᒪᒻᒪᖕᒐᑕ ᑎᒍᔭᐅᓯᒪᕕᒻᒥᓂᕐᒥᓂᒃ, ᑎᒍᔭᐅᓯᒪᔫᑦ ᐃᓄᐃᑦ ᓯᕗᓕᖅᐸᐅᔨᕙᑦᑐᑦ ᓴᓇᙳᐊᓂᕐᒥᒃ, ᐊᒻᒪᓗ ᑐᔪᐃᖅᑕᕈᒪᓪᓗᑎᒃ ᑭᓇᐅᔭᒥᒃ ᐃᓚᒥᓄᑦ. ᐊᒥᓱᑲᓪᓚᐃᓪᓗ ᐃᓄᐃᑦ ᑭᓇᐅᔭᒥᒃ ᐊᐅᓚᑎᔾᔪᑦ ᑎᒍᔭᐅᓯᒪᕕᒻᒥ ᑐᔪᐃᔪᓐᓇᖅᑎᑕᐅᓪᓗᑎᒃ ᓴᓇᐅᒐᐃᕈᑎᒥᓂᕐᒥᓂᒃ.

ᐃᓄᐃᓪᓗ ᑎᒍᔭᐅᓯᒪᔫᑦ ᓴᓇᙳᐊᕈᑎᒥᓂᒃ ᐅᕝᕙᓗ ᓄᑖᓂᒃ ᐱᒍᒪᒍᑎᒃ ᓂᐅᕕᕈᓐᓇᐸᑦᑐᑦ ᑭᓇᐅᔭᓕᐅᕈᑎᒋᓯᒪᔭᒥᓐᓄᓗ. ᐃᓄᐃᑦ ᓴᓇᙳᐊᐸᑦᑐᑦ ᑎᒍᔭᐅᓯᒪᕕᒻᒥ ᓇᒻᒥᓂᖅ ᐊᑭᓖᑦᑐᑦ ᐊᐅᓚᖅᑯᓪᓗᒍ ᑕᒪᓐᓇ ᓴᓇᙳᐊᖅᑕᕐᓂᖅ ᓴᓇᙳᐊᕈᑎᑕᕈᒪᑉᐸᑕᓗ ᑎᑭᓴᐃᓗᑎᒃ ᓇᒻᒥᓂᖅ ᐊᑭᓕᖅᑐᒍᓗ. ᑲᑎᒪᐃᓐᓇᐸᑦᑐᑎᓪᓗ ᓴᓇᙳᐊᖅᑏᑦ ᐃᓄᐃᑦ ᑎᒍᔭᐅᓯᒪᕕᒻᒥ ᒪᓕᒐᒻᒥᓂᒃ ᐊᓯᖕᒋᓐᓂᓪᓗ ᐊᐅᓚᓂᖕᒐᓂᒃ ᐱᔾᔪᑎᖃᑦᑐᑎᒃ.

ᐅᖕᒐᓯᑦᑐᐊᓗᒻᒦᖕᒐᕐᓯᒪᓪᓗᑎᒃ, ᑐᖕᒐᕕᖃᑦᑎᐊᖅᑐᑦ ᐃᓕᖅᑯᓯᒥᓂᒃ ᓴᓇᙳᐊᓂᒃᑯᑦ. ᓴᓇᙳᐊᒐᕐᒥᒍᑦ ᐃᖅᑲᐃᔪᑎᓕᐅᐸᒻᒪᑕ ᓇᑭᖕᒐᓯᒪᓂᕐᒥᓂ ᐃᓅᓯᕐᒥᒍᑦ, ᐊᖕᒐᑯᖕᒍᐊᑎᒍᑦ, ᖃᓄᑎᒋᒃ ᐊᔅᓯᕈᓐᓇᖅᑎᒋᖃᑦᑕᕐᓯᒪᒻᒫᖕᒐᖅ ᓄᓇᒥ, ᐅᒪᔪᐃᑦ ᓄᓇᒥᐅᑕᐃᑦ ᐊᒻᒪᓗ ᐃᒪᕐᒥᐅᑕᐃᑦ, ᒪᓐᓂᓕᐊᕐᓂᒃᑯᑦ, ᐊᐃᕕᐊᕐᓂᖅ, ᑐᑦᑐᐃᑦ ᑐᒥᖕᒋᑦ. ᑐᖕᒐᕕᖃᓐᓂᖕᒋᓐᓂᒃ ᑕᐃᒫᒃ ᐃᓄᐃᑦ ᐱᖅᑯᓯᒥᒍᑦ ᒪᓕᓪᓗᒍ ᑎᒍᔭᐅᓯᒪᕕᐅᑉ ᐃᓗᐊᓂ. ᑕᒪᓐᓇ ᑕᑯᓐᓈᖅᑐᒍ, ᑎᒍᔭᐅᓯᒪᕕᒻᒥ ᐃᖅᑲᓇᐃᔭᖅᑏᑦ ᑐᑭᓯᕙᓪᓕᖅᓯᒪᕗᑦ ᐃᓄᐃᑦ ᒥᔅᓵᓄᑦ ᖃᓄᖅ ᐱᔪᓐᓇᖅᑎᓯᒻᒪᖔᑕ.

ᓯᐅᕕᐊ ᐳᐊᑕᓐ

INTRODUCTION TO THE CARVING PROGRAM

The Fenbrook Inuit Arctic Carving Cooperative was established at Fenbrook to provide the opportunity to the Inuit offenders to create soapstone sculptures for the wholesale art market. By carving to art market standards the Inuit improve their carving skills and become acutely aware of the demands of that market.

When released after sentence to his home community, the Inuit Carver's potential economic contribution to his household income is improved because he has worked at developing his technical and marketing skills. The commissions earned through his carving proceeds are kept in a savings account for his future release.

When asked what they wanted to accomplish while at Fenbrook, the first group of Inuit offenders said that they wanted to carve, and they wanted to send money home to their families. A number of Inuit Carvers have received Warden approval to send money home from their savings earned from carving.

An Inuit can receive approval to replace or purchase new carving tools from his earnings. The Inuit Carving Group pays for all the costs of running the Carving Cooperative, including courier shipping costs, and replacement tools. The Carvers meet regularly to develop policy and procedures for the operations of their Carving enterprise.

Many long miles from home, the Inuit Carvers through their carving remain rooted in the Inuit tradition. The carvings reflect the home life of the hamlets, the magic Shaman transformation, the struggle on the land, the familiar animals of land and sea, the nesting birds, the lumbering walrus, the big-footed caribou.

Thus is established a grounding for the Inuit in his culture within the corrections setting. Observing this, the Fenbrook staff have gained an enriched understanding of this truly remarkable group of people, the Inuit.

Sylvia Purdon
Private Sector Liaison

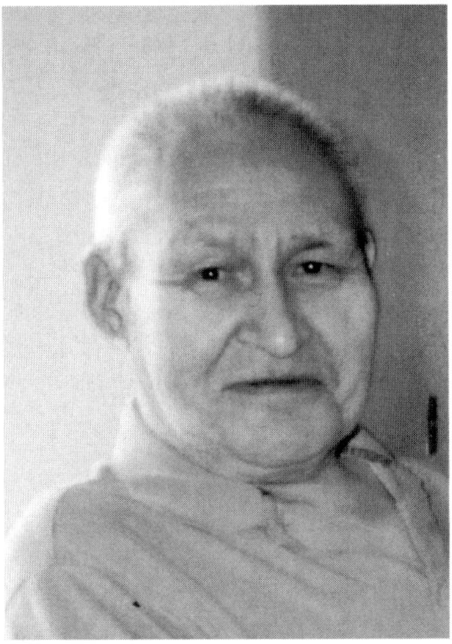

ᑎᒧᑎ ᔮ

ᐃᓄᓚᐅᓯᒪᔪᖓ 1934-ᖑᑎᓪᓗᒍ ᓴᓪᓕᓂ. ᓴᓇᖑᐊᓂᕐᒥᒃ ᐱᒋᐊᓕᓚᐅᓯᒪᔪᖓ 21-ᓂ ᐊᕐᕋᒍᕐᑲᓕᕋᒪ. ᓯᕗᓪᓕᕐᐹᒥ ᓴᓇᖑᐊᓄᐅᕈᑎᒋᓚᐅᓯᒪᔭᕋ ᑐᒑᓕᒃ. ᖁᕕᐊᒋᔭᕋ ᓴᐅᓂᕐᓂᒃ ᓴᓇᖑᐊᓄᐊᓴᖅ ᐱᔾᔪᑎᒋᓪᓗᒍ ᐳᔪᕐᓗᖕᒋᓐᓂᓴᐅᒻᒪᑕ ᐅᑯᓯᓴᔭᓂᒃ. ᓴᓇᖑᐊᖕᒋᓂᓴᐅᕙᑦᑐᖓ ᐅᒃᑯᓯᓴᔭᓂᒃ ᓴᓇᖑᐊᕋᐃᒐᒪ ᖃᓂᒪᔭᓕᓱᖑᒐᒪ ᐳᔪᕐᓗᖓᓄᑦ. ᑭᓯᐊᓂ ᖁᕕᐊᒋᔭᕋ ᒥᑭᔪᑎᓂᒃ ᓴᓇᔭᓇᐊᓴᖅ ᐅᑯᓯᓴᓂᒃ ᐊᖏᓗᐊᕐᑎᓪᓗᒋᑦ ᐳᔪᓗᖃᓗᐊᖓᑕ. ᓴᓇᖑᐊᖅᑐᓂ ᐅᓪᓗᑭᓐᓂᕐᓴᐅᕙᒻᒪᑦ ᑭᓱᓕᓇᖏᒐᐃᒪᒪ ᓴᓇᖑᐊᐸᑦᑐᖓ. ᓴᓇᐅᒐᒃᑲ ᓂᐅᕈᑎᒋᒐᐃᒐᒃᑭᑦ ᓴᐅᓃᑦ ᑭᓇᐅᔭᕐᑖᒃᑲ ᐃᓚᖓᓄᑦ ᑐᔾᑎᒋᕙᕐᑕᑲ. 21-ᓂᒃ ᐊᕐᕋᒍᕐᑲᓕᓚᐅᓯᒪᒐᒪ ᓴᓇᖑᐊᐸᓕᕋᒪ ᖁᕕᐊᒋᓪᓗᒍᓗ ᐅᐱᓐᓇᕋᓂ ᑭᓇᐅᔭᓕᐅᕋᐃᒐᒪ ᓂᕿᑕᕈᓐᓇᕐᓯᕙᒃᑲᒪ. ᑎᒍᔭᐅᓯᒪᕕᒻᒥᓕᕐᑎᓪᓗᖓ ᐊᓯᔾᔨᓗᐊᓯᒪᖏᑦᑐᖅ ᓴᓇᖑᐊᓂᕋ.

TIMOTHY JAR

I was born 1934 in Coral Habour, Nunavut. I started carving when I was 21 years old. The first carving that I made was a narwhal. I like to carve bone, because when you carve bone there is no dust. I try to avoid carving soapstone, because when you carve soapstone, a lot of soapstone dust goes into the air and it makes me feel sick. I don't like to carve large soapstone pieces but I like to make small carvings of animals. I think of carving as a pastime, and whenever I am not doing something I carve. I sell the carvings made from bones and send the money to my family. Ever since I was 21 I have been happy carving because I can buy food with the money that I make. My experience in Fenbrook has not changed the way that I carve.

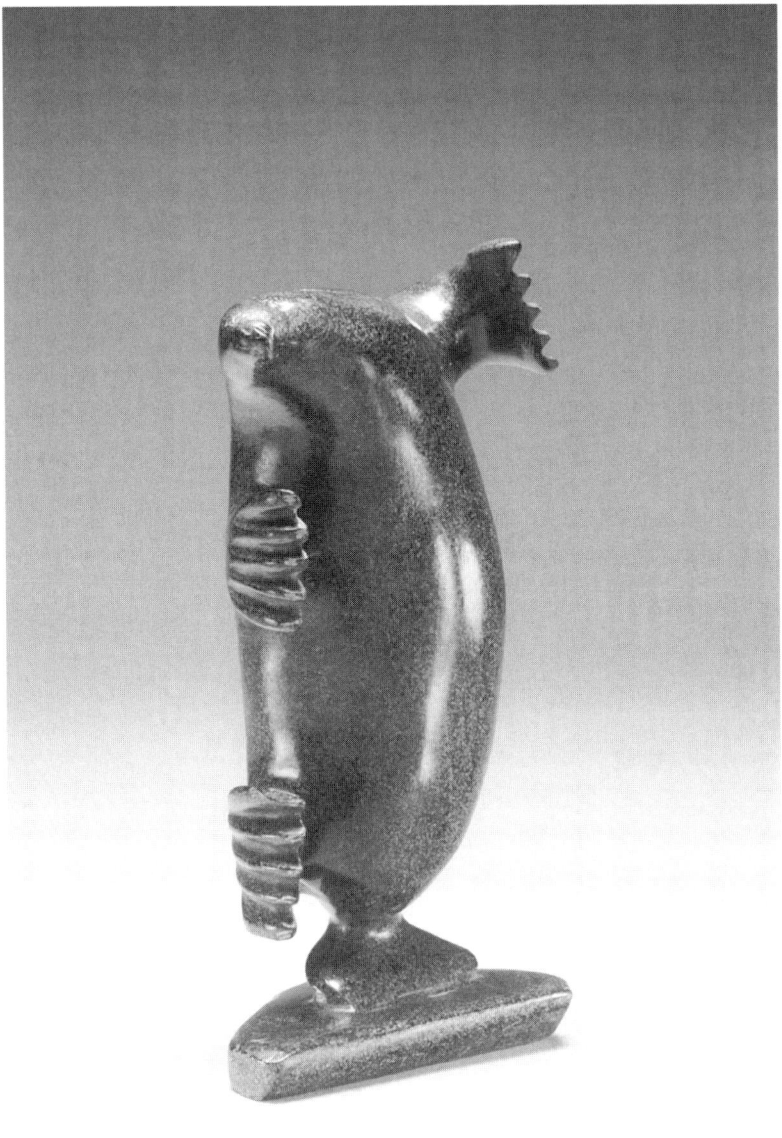

Frolicking Seal, mottled dark grey soapstone, 7"- 17.8 cm

ᐱᖕᒍᐊᑑᒃ ᓇᑦᑏᒃ, ᐃᓱᐊᖕᒐᔪᖅ ᐅᒃᑯᓯᔅᓴᖅ

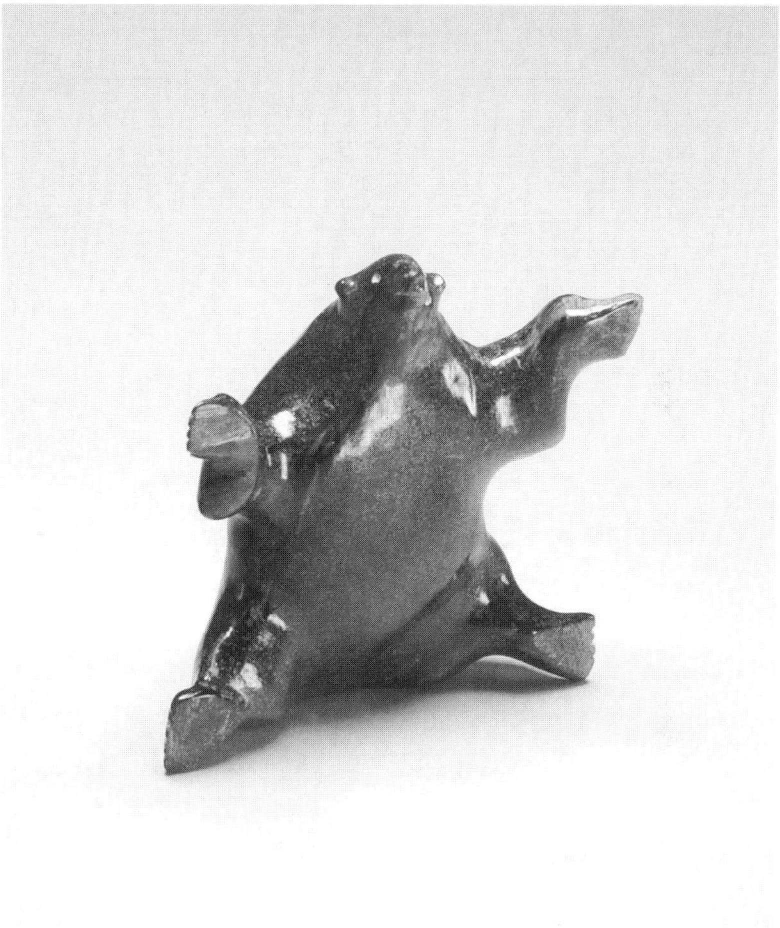

Seated Polar Bear, mottled dark soapstone, 4.5"- 11.4 cm

ᐃᓯᕚᕐᑐᖅ ᓇᓄᖅ, ᕿᓐᓈᖕᒐᔭᖅ ᐅᒃᑯᓯᔅᓴᖅ

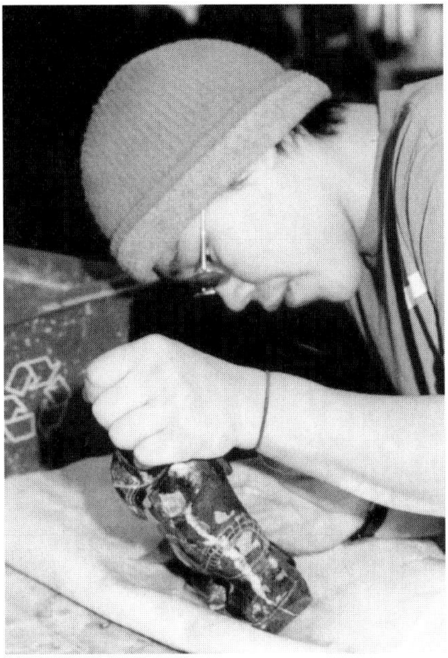

ᑯᓪᓗ ᕿᓕᐸᓕᒃ

ᐊᕐᕋᒍᖅᑲᑦᑐᖓ 20-ᓂᒃ ᑭᓐᖓᓂ ᓄᓇᖅᑲᑦᑐᖓ. ᐱᕈᓴᑎᓪᓗᖓ ᐃᓚᖓᒍᑦ ᐊᔪᓴᑐᓚᐅᕐᑐᒍᑦ, ᑕᐃᒫᒃ ᓴᓇᖑᐊᕋᓱᐸᓕᐊᓕᓚᐅᕐᑐᖓ ᑭᓇᐅᔭᓕᐅᕈᑎᑎᐊᕙᐅᓗᑎᓪᓗ. ᐊᖓᑯᓗᒐ ᐊᒻᒪᓗ ᐋᑕᑕᒐ ᐅᕙᓐᓂᒃ ᓴᓇᖑᐊᕆᐅᓴᑎᑦᑎᓚᐅᖅᓯᒪᔫᒃ. ᖃᐅᔨᒪᔭᐅᑎᐊᕐᑐᑎᓪᓗ ᓴᓇᖑᐊᑎᐅᓂᖏᓐᓄᑦ ᐊᖏᔪᑯᓗᒐᓗ ᓴᓇᖑᐊᑎᐅᒥᔪᑕᐅᖅ. ᓱᕈᓯᐅᓪᓗᖓ ᐋᑕᑕᒐ ᑕᑯᓐᓇᕐᐸᓚᐅᓯᒪᒐᒃᑯ ᐅᑯᓯᔅᓴᒥᒃ ᓴᓇᖑᐊᑎᓪᓗᒍ. ᐃᓛᓐᓂᑯᓪᓗ ᐅᖅᑲᐅᑎᕙᑦᑐᓂᖓ ᐃᒫᒃ ᓴᓇᖑᐊᑎᕈᕈᕕᑦ, ᑐᐊᕕᐅᑎᔭᓗᒥᓗᒍ ᓴᓇᖑᐊᖅᑲᑦᑕᓛᖏᓚᑎᑦ ᓴᓇᑎᐊᓯᒪᓂᓴᐅᖅᑲᑕᓚᖕᒪᑕ. ᐅᕙᓐᓂᒃ ᓴᓇᖑᐊᕆᐅᓴᑎᑎᓕᕋᐃᒻᒪᑦ ᑕᑯᓐᓇᖑᐊᐸᓚᐅᓯᒪᔪᖓ ᓴᓇᖑᐊᑎᓚᕆᐊᓗᑦᓗᖓ ᐅᑯᓯᓴᓂᒃ. 9 ᐅᕝᕙᓗ 10-ᓂᒃ ᐊᕋᒍᖅᑲᑦᑐᖓ ᓴᓇᖑᐊᕆᐅᕈᑎᒥᓚᐅᓯᒪᔭᕋ ᓇᑎᖑᐊᖅ. ᑭᖓᕐᓂ ᐋᑦᑎᒐᓱᕈᓗᔭᐸᔪᔪᖓ ᓴᓇᖑᐊᑕᒥᓂᓐᓂᒃ ᐃᓕᓴᐃᔨᓄᑦ, ᑭᓯᐊᓂ ᓂᐅᕕᐊᖑᖏᒪᑦ. ᐸᓕᓯᒃᑯᓄᑕᓕᕆᕗᖓ, ᐸᓕᓯᐅᑉ ᓂᐅᕕᐊᕆᓚᐅᓯᒪᔭᖓ ᓯᕗᓪᓕᕐᐹᒥ ᓴᓇᖑᐊᕆᐅᕈᑎᖓ 45.00ᒧᑦ ᑕᐃᓱᒪᓂᓕ ᐊᑭᑐᔪᐊᓗᓚᐅᓯᒪᔪᖅ. ᓴᓇᖑᐊᖏᓐᓇᖅᑲᑦᑕᓚᐅᕐᑐᖓ ᐅᑯᓯᓴᓂᒃ ᓄᖅᑲᖓᓕᔪᒥᔪᖓ ᐊᕐᕋᒍᓂᒃ ᐱᖓᓱᓂᒃ.

KUDLU KELLYPALIK

I am 20 years old and I'm from Cape Dorset, Nunavut. When we were growing up we were kind of poor, so I started carving because it was a good way for me to make money. My dad and uncle taught me how to carve. They are famous carvers and my brother is a carver. When I was a kid, I used to watch my father when he was carving soapstone. Sometimes he would tell me, "when you become a carver, don't carve too fast, so there will be more detail in the carving." When he was teaching me I used to imagine my future as a famous soapstone carver. When I was nine or ten years old I did my first soapstone carving of a seal. I went around the community in Cape Dorset to try and sell my piece to the teachers, but they didn't buy it. I went to the R.C.M.P. station and the police officer bought my first carving for $5.00. That money was very big as the time. I kept carving soapstone carvings for a while, but then I stopped for three years.

I remember when I started carving again. My brother was carving a piece in the furnace room, and he told me to leave the room, but I told him I wanted to start carving again, and he said, "go right ahead." I made the head of a seal, and sold it to a small store called Polar Supplies for $5.00. I have been carving soapstone ever since. I have carved bone, antler and ivory. I like to carve in ivory, but most of my carvings are in soapstone. I like to carve dancing seals, masks, and other wild traditional animals. My artwork tells a story. For the Inside Out Charity Auction I made a carving about a woman and child in a fashion show. It represented the way we are losing our traditional culture. The fashion show was a symbol of modern society. The carving tells the story of a woman standing with her hands inside the front of her parka, and there is her child at her side wearing a baby parka. The child is scared of the fashion show and she is crying. Another carving I did was of a polar bear and seal dancing. They are dancing because they are happy that they still exist, happy to be celebrating instead of killing each other.

ᐃᖅᑲᐅᒪᔪᖕᒐ ᓴᓇᖕᒍᐊᖅᑲᑦᑕᑲᓐᓂᓕᖃᒪ. ᐊᖕᒋᔪᑯᓗᒐ ᓴᓇᖕᒍᐊᓚᐅᓯᒪᒻᒪᑦ ᐅᖅᑯᓴᐅᑎᖅᑲᕕᒻᒥ, ᐅᐸᑯ ᐊᓂᖅᑯᓪᓗᒐ ᑕᕝᕙᖕᒐᑦ, ᐅᖅᑲᐅᑎᓪᓗᒍ ᓴᓇᖕᒍᐊᖅᑲᑦᑕᑲᓐᓂᕈᒪᓕᖃᒪ ᐅᖅᑲᐅᑎᓪᓗᖕᒐ ᓴᓇᖕᒍᐊᓕᕆᑦ. ᓇᑎᐅᑉ ᓂᐊᖅᑯᖕᒍᐊᖕᒐᓂᒃ ᓴᓇᓕᓚᐅᓯᒪᔪᖕᒐ, ᐊᓱᐃᓪᓚᓗ ᓂᐅᕕᐊᖕᒍᓪᓗᓂ ᓂᐅᕕᖅᕕᖃᓛᕈᓗᒻᒍᑦ ᐊᑎᓕᒃ ᐹᓗ ᑭᓱᕈᓗᔪᑯᕕᖕᒐ ᐊᑭᖅᑲᑦᑐᓂ ᓴᓇᖕᒍᐊᒐᖃ 45.00ᒥᒃ. ᑕᐃᒪᖕᒐᓂᒃ ᓴᓇᖕᒍᐊᖕᒋᓐᓇᖅᐸᓕᖅᑐᖕᒐ. ᓴᓇᖕᒍᐊᖅᑲᑦᑕᖅᓯᒪᓕᖅᑐᖕᒐ ᓴᐅᓂᖅᓂᒃ, ᓇᔾᔭᓂᒃ ᐊᒻᒪᓗ ᑑᒐᖅᓂᑦ. ᖅᑯᕕᐊᓯᔪᖃ ᓴᓇᖕᒍᐊᕆᐊᓴᖅ ᑑᒐᖅᓂᑦ, ᑭᓯᐊᓂ ᓴᓇᖕᒍᐊᓯᒪᔪᓕᒫᒃᑲ ᐅᑯᓯᔅᓴᔪᐃᓇᐸᓗᐃᑦ. ᖅᑯᕕᐊᓯᔪᖃᓗ ᓴᓇᖕᒍᐊᕆᐊᓴᖅ ᑖᓂᓯᖕᒍᐊᖅᑐᓂᒃ ᓇᑎᖕᒍᐊᓂᒃ, ᑮᓇᖕᒍᐊᓂᒃ ᐊᒻᒪᓗ ᐆᒪᔪᖕᒍᐊᓂᒃ. ᓴᓇᖕᒍᐊᕆᐊᓚᐅᓐᓇᒍ ᐅᑯᓯᔅᓴᖅ, ᓂᕆᕕᐅᑉ ᖅᑲᖕᒐᓄᓚᐅᖅᑐᒍ ᖅᑭᒥᕈᑕᓕᖅᑲᖃ ᐊᒻᒪᓗ ᑕᑯᓐᓇᖕᒍᐊᖃᓱᑕᓕᖅᑯᖕᒐ ᖅᑲᓄᖅ ᓴᓇᖕᒍᐊᓂᐊᒪᖕᒑᒃᑯ. ᐃᓛᓐᓂᒃᑯᑦ ᐊᑯᓂᐊᓗᒃ ᐃᓱᒪᓴᓯᐅᖅᖃᓱᓐᓇᑐᖅ ᖅᑲᓄᐃᓕᖕᒐᓂᐊᖅᒪᖕᒑᖅ. ᑎᒍᔪᐅᓯᒪᕕᒻᒥᓕᖅᑎᓪᓗᖕᒐ ᓴᓇᖕᒍᐊᕆᐅᑲᓂᖅᓯᒪᔪᖕᒐ ᖅᑲᓄᐃᓕᐅᓯᒪᓂᖅᓴᐅᓗᑎᓪᓗ. ᒫᓐᓇ ᓴᓇᖕᒍᐊᐸᑦᑕᖃ ᖅᑭᓂᖅᑕᐅᓗᓂ ᐃᓛᓐᓂᑯᓪᓗ ᐃᖅᑭᐊᓇᓯᑲᐃᓇᐸᑦᑐᓂ ᐊᔾᔨᒋᖕᒋᓐᓈᓗᒻᒥᒃ ᐅᑯᓯᔅᒥᒃ ᓴᓇᖕᒍᐊᓇᐊᓴᖅ. ᓘᓇᑎᓐᓂᓕ ᐅᑯᓯᔅᓴᓂᒃ ᐊᔨᖕᒋᑦᑐᓂᒃ ᐱᑕᖅᑲᓐᓂᓴᐅᒻᒪᑦ. ᖅᑯᕕᐊᓯᔪᖃ ᓴᓇᖕᒍᐊᓇᐊᓴᖅ ᖅᑯᔪᓐᓇᒥᓯᒪᔪᖃ ᐊᑖᑕᒐ, ᐊᖕᒋᔪᑯᓗᒐ ᑭᖕᒍᓪᓕᖅᐹᒥᑦᓗ ᐊᖕᒐᑯᓗᒐ, ᑐᓂᔪᐅᓯᒪᒐᒪ ᐃᓕᑦᑎᑕᐅᓯᒪᓪᓗᖕᒐᓗ ᓴᓇᖕᒍᐊᓂᖅᒥᒃ.

Before I begin carving, I put the soapstone on the table and look at it and try to imagine the shape of the stone and what I can carve it into. Sometimes it takes a long time to decide what shape the stone should be. In Fenbrook I have improved my carvings because I am putting in more details. The stone that I have been using is black, and sometimes it can be boring to carve the same colour of stone. At home I can carve any kind of stone. I enjoy carving, and I am thankful to my father, my older brother, and lastly to my uncle for giving the gift to be a creative carver. I think that carving is really important; if I had a child I would teach him to carve to keep our traditions that have been taught before. When I was at home I taught some children how to carve, and they would watch while my brother and I would carve every day. I would tell them to teach carving to others when they grow up, to show how we do hard work all the time, and to pass on the cultural traditions.

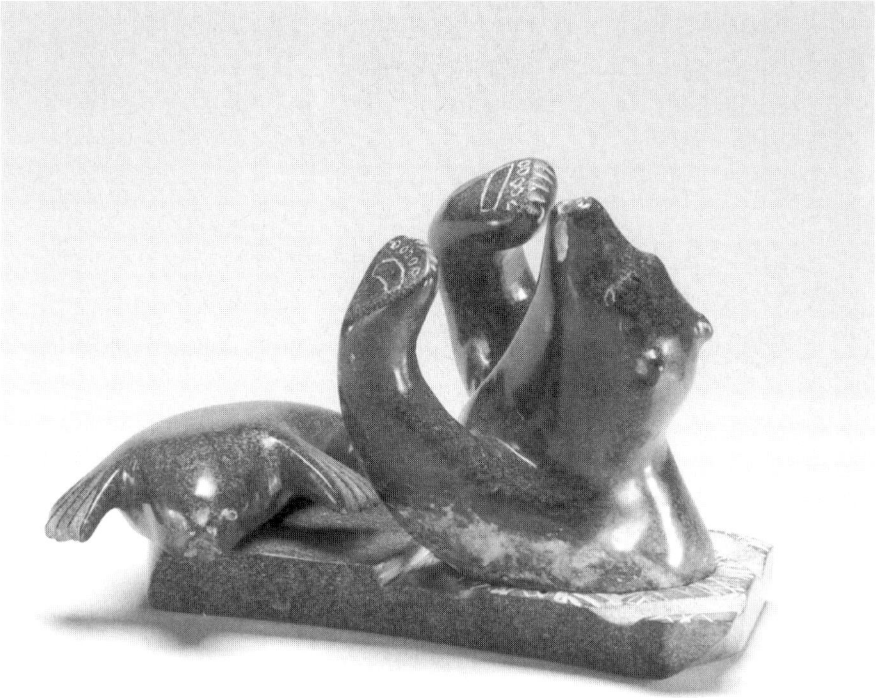

Polar Bear attacking a Seal on an Ice Floe, mottled grey soapstone, 8"- 20.3 cm

ᓇᓄᖅ ᓇᑦᑎᓕᕐᑐᖅ ᓯᓈᖕᒐᓂ, ᑐᖕᒍᔪᕈᔪᑦᑐᖅ ᐅᒃᑯᓯᔅᓴᖅ

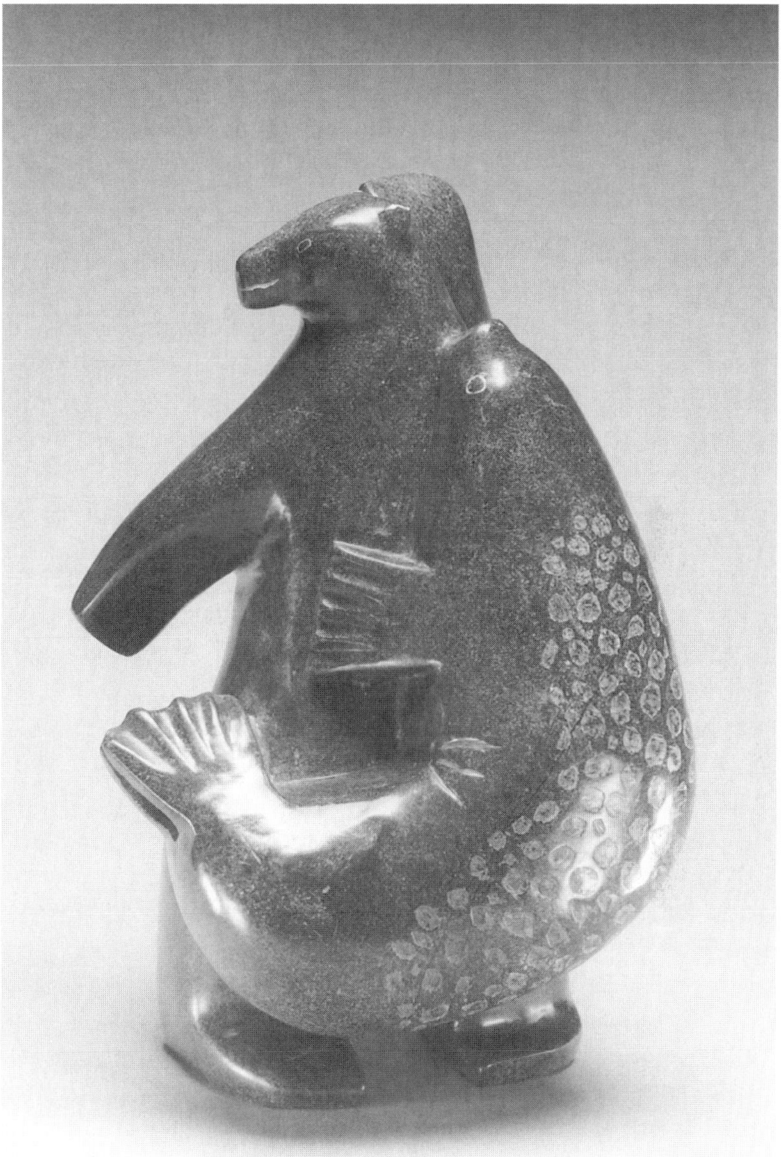

Polar Bear dancing with a Seal, mottled dark grey soapstone, 17"- 43.2 cm

ᓇᓄᖅ ᑕᓃᓯᖅᑎᓕᒃ ᓇᑦᑎᕐᒥᒃ, ᐃᓱᐊᖕᒪᔪᖅ ᐅᒃᑯᓯᔅᓴᖅ

ᔪᐊᓇᓯ ᑲᒃᑭᒃ ᖁᐊᕋᖅ

ᓄᓇᖃᑦᑐᖓ ᐃᖃᓗᓐᓂ ᓄᓇᕘᒥ. 29-ᓂᒃ ᐊᕐᕌᒍᖃᑦᑐᖓ. ᐊᕙᑎᑲᓴᓐᓂᒃ ᐊᕐᕌᒍᓂᒃ ᓴᓇᖑᐊᕐᑎᐅᓕᖅᑐᖓ. ᐃᖅᑲᐅᒪᔪᖓ 9-ᓂᒃ ᐊᕋᒍᖃᑦᑐᖓ ᓴᓇᖑᓚᐅᓯᒪᒐᒪ ᓯᕗᓪᓕᕐᐸᒥ, ᓇᑎᖑᐊᓕᐅᓚᐅᓯᒪᒐᒪ ᒥᑭᔪᕈᓗᒻᒥᒃ. ᐱᒡᒐᓇᓚᐅᖅᓯᒪᔪᖅ ᓯᕗᓕᕐᐸᒥ ᓴᓇᖑᐊᕋᓯᐊᕐᑐᓂ, ᑭᓯᐊᓂ ᐊᑖᑕᒪ ᐃᑲᔪᕐᑐᓂᖓ ᐱᔮᕆᐸᓚᐅᓯᒪᔪᖓ. ᐊᑖᑕᒐ ᐅᕙᓐᓂᒃ ᑕᑯᓇᑎᑦᑎᖃᕐᐸᓚᐅᕐᑐᖅ ᓴᓇᖑᐊᕐᑐᓂ ᐊᔪᕆᓲᑎᑦᑕᓕᖅᑳᖓ ᖃᓄᐃᒥᐊᖃᒻᒫᖓᖅᑐ ᐅᖃᐅᑎᕙᑦᑐᓂᖓᑐ, ᑭᓯᐊᓂ ᐃᒻᒥᓂᓇᕿᑎᓐᓂᓴᕆᐸᓚᐅᕐᑳᖓ ᑕᒻᒪᓂᒃᑲ ᐃᓕᓐᓂᐊᕈᑎᒥᓂᐊᕋᒃᕿᑦ. ᐃᖅᑲᐅᒪᐃᓇᓂᐊᕐᑐᖓ ᓯᕗᓪᓕᕐᐸᒥ ᓴᓇᐅᒐᐃᕋᒪ, ᓴᓇᐅᒐᐃᕈᑎᒐ ᑮᓇᐅᔭᖅ Hᐊᑭᓯᑎᑕᕈᑎᒋᓚᐅᓯᒪᒐᒃᑯ ᐅᕙᓐᓄᑦ ᐊᓈᓇᓐᓄᑦᑐ ᓂᐅᕕᓚᐅᖅᓯᒪᒐᒪ. ᐃᖅᑲᐅᒪᒻᒥᔪᖓ ᐊᑖᑕᒐ ᑕᑯᑎᒍᒪᓚᐅᖅᓯᒪᒐᒃᑯ ᓴᓇᖑᐊᕈᓐᓇᓕᕋᒪ ᐊᖏᔪᖅᑲᖓᓄᑦᑐ ᓂᐅᕈᑎᒥᔪᓐᓇᕐᓯᒪᒐᒃᑯ. ᐊᑖᑕᒐ ᐅᐱᒍᓱᕐᑯᓚᐅᓯᒪᒐᒃᑯ ᑕᐃᒪᑕᐅᖅ ᐊᑖᑕᒐᑎᑐᑦ ᓴᓇᖑᐊᕈᓐᓇᓕᕋᒪ. ᑕᐃᒪᖓᓂᒃ ᓴᓇᖑᐊᑎᕈᕈᒪᓚᐅᓯᒪᔪᖓ ᓯᕗᓪᓕᕐᐸᒥ ᓴᓇᖑᐊᕆᐅᕈᑎᓐᓄᑦ. ᐃᖅᑲᐅᒪᒥᔪᖓ ᓱᕈᓯᐅᓪᓗᖓ ᓄᐊᑎᓚᐅᓯᒪᒐᒪ ᖃᓄᐃᓕᐅᑐᖃᕈᓗᔭᕐᓂᐊᑎᓪᓗᒍ ᐆᑐᑎᒥᓗᒍ ᐃᓄᐃᑦ ᐱᖑᐊᕈᓯᖏᓐᓂᒃ ᐊᒻᒪᓗ Hᐊᑭᕐᑐᓂᒃ ᑕᑯᓐᓇᕆᐊᖅ ᐅᕝᕙᓗ ᐊᓐᓂᑭᑦᑐᐊᔪᒥᐊᖅᑐᕐᑐᖓ. ᐃᓄᓯᑦᑐᓂᓕᒫᓐᓂ ᐃᖅᑲᓇᐃᔭᖅᑲᑦᑕᕐᓯᒪᔪᖓ ᐊᒻᒪᓗ ᓴᓇᖑᐊᐸᑦᑐᖓ ᐃᓚᒃᑲ ᐃᑲᔪᕋᓯᐊᕐᑐᒥᑦ. ᓴᓇᖑᐊᓂᕐᓴᓇᕙᑦᑕᒃᑲ ᐅᑯᓯᔅᓴᐃᑦ ᑭᓯᐊᓂ ᐃᓚᓐᓂᒃᑯᑦ ᑑᒐᕐᒥᒃ ᓴᓇᖑᐊᐸᒻᒥᔪᖓ ᐊᑐᕆᐊᖃᕋᐃᒐᒃᑯ ᓴᓇᖑᐊᒐᓐᓄᑦ. ᐊᑖᑕᒪ ᐊᔪᕆᓯᐅᑎᕙᔪᒻᒫᖓ ᐅᑯᓯᔅᓴᖅ ᑕᑯᓐᓇᖅᑳᓚᐅᒃᑐᒍ, ᐅᖃᑉᐸᔪᒻᒪᓪᓗ ᑕᑯᔪᓐᓇᓯᓛᕋᒪ ᐅᑯᓯᔅᓴᖅ ᐃᓗᐊ ᖃᓄᐃᑐᕈᕈᓐᓇᕐᓂᖓᓂᒃ.

ᓴᓇᖑᐊᐸᑦᑕᒃᑲ ᑎᒍᔭᐅᓯᒪᕕᒻᒥ ᐃᓚᒍᑎᒥᒃᑲᓂᕐᓯᒪᔭᒃᑲ ᐊᕿᓐᓂᓴᐅᒻᒪᑕᓗ ᓴᓇᖑᐊᕆᐊᖏᑕ. ᐊᒻᒪᓗ ᐃᓚᑲᓂᕐᓯᒪᓪᓗᖓ ᐊᓯᓐᓂᒃ. ᐊᐱᕐᓱᑐᖓᓗ Hᐊᒥᒃ ᐃᓐᓇᑐᖃᐃᑦ ᐃᓚᖓᓐᓂᒃ, ᐊᖑᓇᓱᒍᑎᐅᖃᑦᑕᓚᐅᓯᒪᔪᑦ ᐅᐊᑎᐊᕈ ᒥᔅᓵᓄᑦ ᐊᒻᒪᓗ ᐃᓄᓯᖑᐊᓂᒃ ᓴᓇᖑᐊᓂᐊᓗᑎᒃ ᖃᓄᖅ ᐱᕙᓐᓂᒫᖓᑕ. ᖁᕕᐊᒋᔭᕋᓗ ᐃᓄᐃᑦ ᐱᖅᑯᓯᖏᓐᓂᒃ ᓴᓇᖑᐊᕆᐊᓴᖅ. ᐃᓛᓐᓂᒃᑯᑦ ᕿᒥᕐᕈᐊᕈᓗᔭᐸᑦᑐᖓ ᕿᒥᕐᕈᐊᒐᓐᓂᒃ ᐃᓱᒪᑖᕐᐸᓕᐊᒍᑎᒥᓂᐊᕿᑦ ᓴᓇᖑᐊᓕᕈᒪ, ᑭᓯᐊᓂ ᐃᓱᒪᒋᔭᒃᑲ ᒪᓕᓐᓂᓴᕆᑦᑕᑲ. ᓴᓇᖑᐊᑎᐅᖃᑎᒃᑲ ᐃᓕᓐᓂᐊᕐᑎᓯᒪᒥᔭᒃᑲ ᖃᓄᖅ ᓴᓇᖑᐊᓂᕐᒥᒃ. ᓴᓇᖑᐊᓂᖅ ᐅᕙᓐᓂᒃ ᖁᕕᐊᓱᓕᖅᑎᑦᑎᕙᑦᑐᖅ,

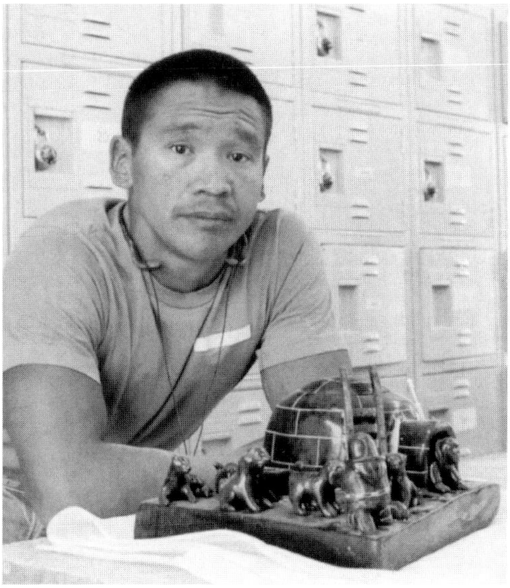

JOANASIE KORGAK

I am from Iqaluit, Nunavut. I'm 29 years of age. I've been carving for almost 20 years. I recall making a first carving at the age of nine. I made a small seal. It was difficult to carve at first, but with help from my father I completed it. He would let me watch him carve and then tell me what to do, but he made me carve by myself because he knew I would learn by making my own mistakes. I will always remember selling my first carving, because with the money that I made I was able to buy myself a hockey stick and a gift for my mother. Before I first made a carving, I recall I wanted to show that I could make one and sell it to my father's boss. I wanted my father to be happy that I could do the same as him. I've always wanted to be a carver ever since I made my first carving. When I was young I remember gathering together for special occasions like playing Inuit games and going to watch hockey and going skating. All my teenage life I worked and carved to support my family. I mostly carve soapstone but

ᐃᓱᒪᑦᑎᐊᕆᑎᑎᓪᓗᓂ, ᓴᓇᖑᐊᓕᕋᐃᒐᒪ ᖁᕕᐊᒋᔭᕋ ᑐᓴᕋᓐᓈᕆᐊᔅᓴᖅ ᓂᔾᔮᔪᓂᒃ. ᖃᐅᔨᒪᔭᐅᓕᕈᒪᔪᖓ ᓴᓇᖑᐊᑎᐅᓂᓐᓄᑦ. ᐅᓪᓗᒥᐅᓕᕐᑐᖅ ᓴᓇᖑᐊᒐᒃᑲ ᐱᐅᓰᕙᓕᖅᓯᒪᔪᑦ. ᐱᐅᒋᒐᒃᑯ ᖃᓄᕐᑐᕋᕈᓗᔭᕆᐊᓴᖅ ᐊᒻᒪᓗ ᑕᑯᓴᐅᑎᑦᑎᒋᐊᔅᓴᖅ ᐃᓄᐃᑦ ᐱᖅᑯᓯᖏᓐᓂᒃ ᓴᓇᖑᐊᓂᒃᑯᑦ, ᓰᕐᓗ ᐆᑦᑐᑎᒋᓗᒍ ᐃᓄᐃᑦ ᐱᖑᐊᕈᓯᖏᑦ ᓄᓯᕋᐅᑎᖑᐊᕐᑐᑦ ᐅᕝᕙᓗ ᐃᕿᒥᓄᑦ ᐱᖑᐊᕐᑐᑦ. ᓴᓇᖑᐊᖅᓯᒪᒻᒥᔪᖓ ᒪᕐᕉᒃ ᐊᕐᓈᒃ ᑲᑕᔾᔭᖑᐊᕐᑑᒃ, ᐊᖑᑏᒃ ᐃᕿᒥᒍᑦ ᐱᖑᐊᕐᑑᒃ, ᐊᒻᒪᓗ ᑮᓇᖑᐊᖅ ᐸᑎᐅᔭᒃᑯᕕᐅᓗᓂ. ᐱᐅᒋᓂᕐᐹᕆᓯᒪᔭᕋ ᓴᓇᖑᐊᖅᓯᒪᔭᓐᓂᒃ ᐃᖕᒋᕋᔭᕕᒃ ᐃᓚᒌᖑᐊᑦ ᐃᓄᖑᐊᑦ ᕿᒧᔅᓯᖑᐊᕐᑐᑦ. ᒫᓐᓇ ᓴᓇᖑᐊᕐᒥᔪᖓ ᒪᕐᕉᒃ ᐃᓄᖑᐊᒃ ᐃᓄᐃᑦ ᐱᖑᐊᕈᓯᖓᓂᒃ ᐱᖑᐊᑑᒃ ᐊᑎᓕᒃ ᐅᒥᒪᐅᔭᖅ.

ᓴᓇᖑᐊᑲᕈᐸᓪᓕᐊᔪᖓ ᖃᓄᕈᓘᔭᖅ, ᐱᐅᔪᑎᐅᑦᑐᑎᒃ ᒥᑭᔪᑎᐅᑦᑐᑎᑦᑐ ᐱᔭᕆᑎᐊᓯᒪᕙᑦᑐᑎᑦᑐ ᖃᓄᐃᓕᐅᕈᓗᔭᕐᓯᒪᔪᓂᒃ. ᓴᓇᖑᐊᐸᑦᑐᖓᓗ ᐅᕙᖓ ᐃᓕᖁᓯᖓᓂᖔᖅᓯᒪᔪᒥᒃ. ᓴᓇᖑᐊᕐᑎᐅᑦᑐᓂ ᕿᓄᐃᓴᕆᐊᖃᓐᓂᕐᒥᒃ ᐱᓯᒪᔭᕆᐊᖃᓐᓇᕐᑐᖅ. ᓯᓚᕐᔪᐊᓕᒫᕐᒧᑦ ᓴᓇᖑᐊᒐᒃᑲ ᖃᐅᔨᔭᐅᓛᕐᑯᔭᒃᑲ

sometimes I use a little bit of ivory for the details in my soapstone carvings. My father taught me to look at the block of soapstone, and he told me that I could see all kinds of carvings inside the block.

The soapstone that I have been working with in Fenbrook has allowed me to do some more shaping because it is softer and it allows me to do some more details. I have also learned from others in the group. I ask one of the elders, like Ham, for some advice how to use the tools properly. I like to use my Inuit traditions in my carving. Sometimes I look through books to give me ideas, but most of my ideas come from my head. I also have instructed some of the other carvers, teaching them ways to carve. Carving makes me happy, it keeps me clear minded, and when I carve I like to listen to music. I want to be a well-known carver. My carvings today have improved. I like to be creative in showing Inuit traditional ways in my carvings, like two individuals playing an Inuit mercy game pulling each other's lips. Some of the carvings that I have made are two women throat-singing, two men competing at the lip-pulling game, and face-masks that are candle-holders. My best carving was a chess-piece family with a dog team. I am working on a carving of two individuals playing an Inuit game called Musk-Ox fight.

I am going to be creative, making my carvings with nice finishing and with lots of details. I will make carvings that have to do with my culture. As a carver, being patient is the most important skill to achieve. I look forward to showing my artwork to the world.

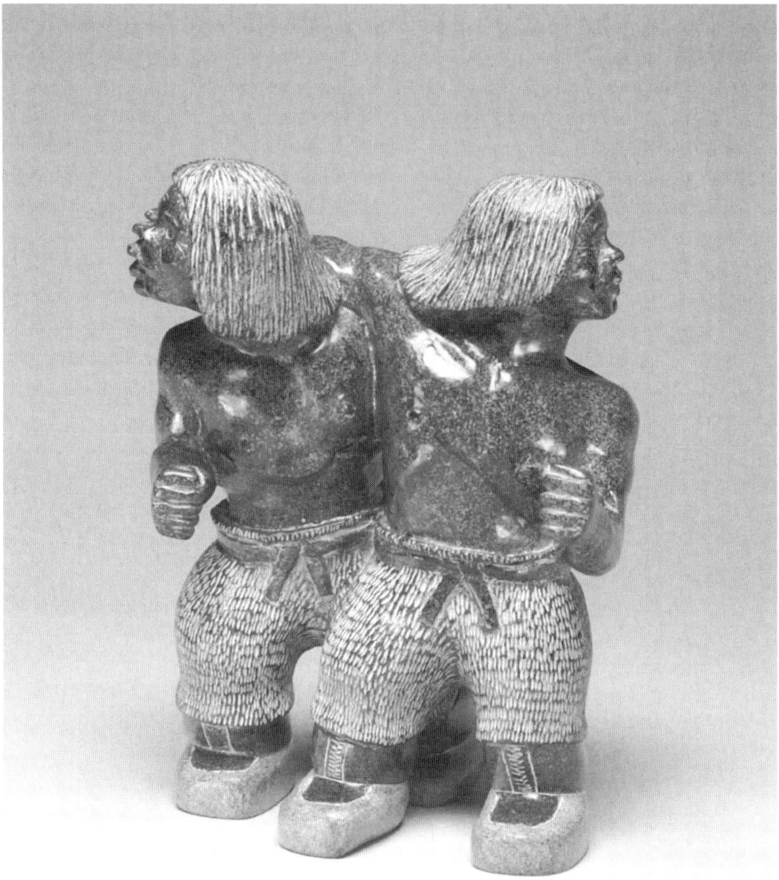

Two Men competing in a lip-mercy event, mottled dark soapstone, 9"- 22.9 cm

ᒪᕐᕉᒃ ᐃᓅᒃ ᐊᖑᑏᒃ ᓴᓚᒥᖃᑕᐅᑎᒐᓱᐊᕐᑑᒃ ᐃᕿᒥᓄᑦ ᐱᖑᐊᑐᑎᒃ, ᕿᓐᓇᖕᒐᔪᖅ ᐅᑯᓯᔅᓴᖅ

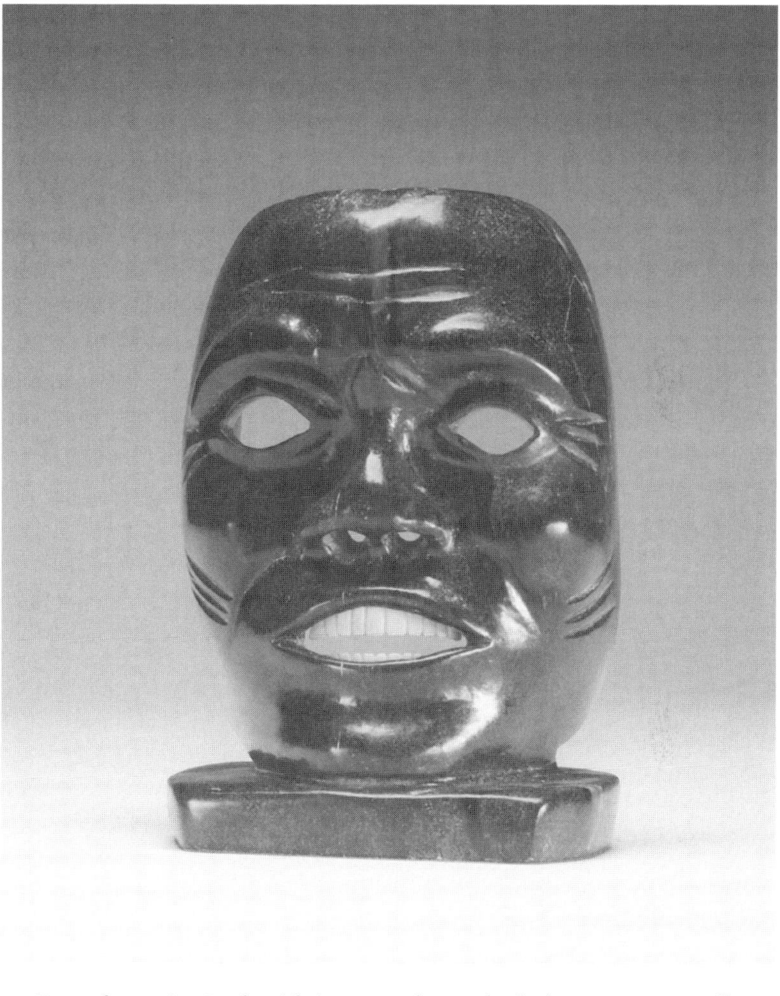

Face of a staring Inuk, with insert antler teeth, dark soapstone candle holder, 8"- 20.3 cm

ᓴᐅᒥᒃ: ᐃᓄᒃ ᐅᑭᔨᑦᑐᓂ ᑕᑯᓐᓇᕐᑐᖅ, ᑭᒍᑎᖕᒋᑦ ᓇᔾᕙᒥᓃᑦ, ᖅᑭᓐᓇᖕᒐᕙᖅ ᐅᒃᑯᓯᔅᓴᖅ ᐸᑎᐅᔭᒃᑯᕕᒃ

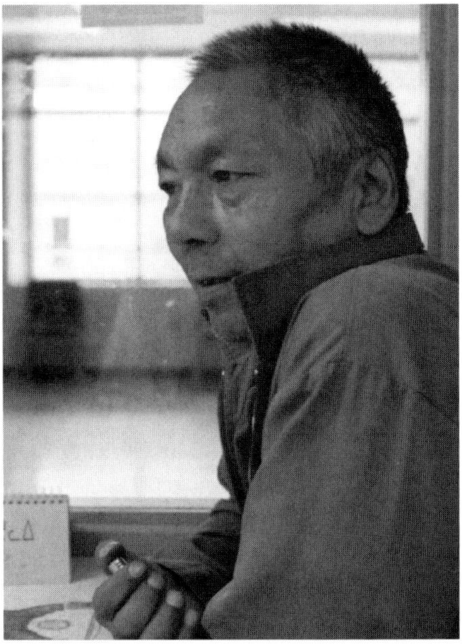

ᒪᓈᐅᓯ ᑭᓪᓗᐊ

ᓇᐅᔫᓂ ᐃᓄᓚᐅᓯᒪᕗᖓ 1949-ᖑᑎᓪᓗᒍ. ᐅᑯᓯᓴᓂᒃ ᓴᓇᖑᐊᖃᑦᑕᓕᓚᐅᓯᒪᕗᖓ 18-ᓂᒃ ᐅᑭᐅᖃᑦᑐᖓ. ᓯᕗᓪᓕᖅᐹᒥ ᓴᓇᖑᐊᓇᐅᕈᑎᒋᓚᐅᓯᒪᔪᕋ ᑎᒻᒥᐊᖑᐊᖅ. ᑕᑯᓐᓇᖃᑦᑕᖅᑐᖓ ᓴᓇᖑᐊᓱᓂᒃ ᓴᓇᖑᐊᑎᓪᓗᒋᑦ. ᐃᓕᓯᒪᒥᕗᖓᓗ ᓴᓇᖑᐊᓂᖅᒥᒃ ᐊᑖᑕᑦᓯᐊᓐᓂᒃ. ᓴᓇᖑᐊᖃᑦᑕᕈᓐᓂᑲᐃᓇᓚᐅᓯᒪᕗᖓ ᐃᖅᑲᓇᐃᔭᓕᕋᒪ, ᐅᔭᕋᓐᓂᐊᖅᑎᓂ. ᐅᐊᑎᐊᕈᑲᓪᓚᐅᓕᖓᑦ ᕿᒥᕈᐊᒐᓂᓕᓚᐅᓯᒪᕗᖅ ᓴᓇᖑᐊᒐᕋ. ᖁᕕᐊᒋᔭᕋ ᓴᓇᖑᐊᓇᐊᓴᖅ ᑯᐊᐸᒃᑯᓐᓄᑦ. ᐃᓕᓴᓇᔪᐅᕙᒪᕗᖅ ᓴᓇᖑᐊᑎᐅᓂᓐᓄᑦ ᓯᓛᕙᐊᕐᒥ. ᐱᐅᑎᒐᓱᐊᑎᐊᕐᑐᒋᑦ ᓴᓇᖑᐊᐸᑦᑐᖓ ᐅᑯᓯᔅᓴᖅ. ᖁᔭᓇᒦᖅᓯᒪᕗᖅ ᐱᕕᖃᑎᑕᐅᒐᒪ ᓴᓇᖑᐊᓂᖅᒥᒃ. ᐊᓯᖏᓐᓂᒃ ᓴᓇᖑᐊᖃᑦᑕᖅᓯᒪᒥᕗᖅ ᐅᒪᕗᒥᓃᑦ ᓴᐅᓂᖏᓐᓂᒃ, ᐆᑦᑐᑎᒋᓗᒍ ᕿᓚᓗᒐᒥᓂᖅ. ᐅᑉᐱᕈᓱᑐᖓ ᓴᓇᖑᐊᒐᒃᑲ ᐱᐅᓯᕆᓪᓕᐊᖏᓐᓇᓂᐊᖓᑕ ᐊᓂᒍᒪᓗ ᑎᒍᔭᐅᓯᒪᕕᒻᒥᒃ ᐱᐅᓂᖅᓴᐅᓕᓚᖓᑕ ᐊᖏᕋᓗᑦ ᐅᑎᕈᒪ. ᐅᖓᓕᑎᐊᖅᑐᖓ ᐅᔭᕿᐊᖃᑕᐅᔭᓇᐊᓴᖅ ᐅᑯᓯᓴᓂᒃ ᖃᓗᕋᖅᑐᓂ ᖃᒧᖓᓗᓪᓗ ᐅᑯᓯᓴᓂᓪᓗ ᐱᓯᖃᑦᑕᐸᓪᓕᐊᓕᖅᑐᓂ ᖁᕕᐊᓇᖓᑦ. ᖁᕕᐊᒋᔭᕋ ᐅᑯᓯᓴᓂᒃ ᓴᓇᖑᐊᓇᐊᓴᖅ, ᐊᓯᖏᓐᓂᓪᓗ ᐆᑦᑐᖃᑦᑕᖅᓯᒪᒥᕗᖅ

MARIUS KRIDLUAR

I was born in Repulse Bay, Nunavut, in 1949. I started to carve soapstone when I was 18. My first carvings were of birds, seals and whales. I began by watching other carvers do their work, learning from them, and as I became more experienced at age 29 I moved on to carving figures. I also learned to carve by watching my grandfather. I would copy his style and techniques. When I was a young boy I really wanted to buy a radio, and my grandfather suggested that I sell my carvings and save the money. The radio was expensive and I had to sell thirty carvings to make enough money to buy it. At the time I was selling my carvings for 30 cents to 2 dollars. I stopped carving when I moved to find work but I was always learning about carving and soapstone. I worked in a gold mine that was in Eskimo Point in the Northwest Territories (at that time) and working there taught me about the different types of soapstone. At the mine there was a wide variety of soapstone that I collected and carved. I worked with some workers who were educated in the science of stones. They would teach me, along with other carvers, what types of soapstone were the best to carve. They taught me that black soapstone was the best soapstone because it was durable. Underwater soapstone, that could be gathered at low tide, was good to carve but you had to be careful because it was fragile and cracked easily. Soft soapstone was more fragile than the soapstone found in water because it has the tendency to chip. Several years later in 1996, I saw my green soapstone carving of an owl in a catalogue book. This was a carving that I had made when I was 19. Seeing my work in the catalogue made my wife and three children and me very happy and proud. We kept the catalogue with the photo of my carving in it and it is still on display in my home today. I like carving for the Arctic Co-operatives Limited and I would like to be recognized widely for my work. I have tried my best to carve soapstone carvings, and I am very thankful to be given the

ᓴᐅᓂᕐᓂᒃ ᐊᒻᒪᓗ ᑑᒐᓂᒃ. ᐱᕆᐊᖅᓲᖕᒍᔪᖕᒐ ᕿᒥᕈᖅᑲᓚᐅᕐᑐᒍ ᓴᓇᖕᒍᐊᒐᓴᖅ ᐃᓱᒪᓴᓯᐅᕈᑎᒋᓪᓗᒍᓗ ᖃᓄᖅ ᓴᓇᖕᒍᐊᓂᐊᕐᒫᖕᒐᒃᑯ, ᑐᑭᑖᕋᐃᒐᒪᓗ ᖃᓄᐃᓕᖕᒐᓂᐊᕐᒫᖕᒐᖅ ᐱᕆᐊᓕᑕᐃᓐᓇᑕᖅᑯᖕᒐ. ᖁᕙᐊᓱᓕᑲᓂᕐᐸᑦᑐᖕᒐ ᓴᓇᖕᒍᐊᓕᕋᐃᒐᒪ. ᖁᕙᐊᕆᓂᕐᐹᕋ ᓴᓇᖕᒍᐊᕐᑐᒍ ᓂᐊᖁᒥᓂᖕᒐ ᐊᐃᕙᐅᑉ. ᖃᑕᖕᒍᑎᒃᑲᑕᐅᖅ ᓴᓇᖕᒍᐊᓱᖕᒍᒻᒥᔪᑦ. ᐅᑉᐱᒍᓱᑦᑐᖕᒐ ᐱᖅᑯᓯᓄᒐᑦᑎᒍ ᓴᓇᖕᒍᐊᕐᓂᖅ ᔭᒐᓚᐅᓯᒪᔮᒐᓂᓗ. ᖁᔭᓕᓪᓚᓇᑦᑐᖕᒐ ᐱᕙᖅᑦᑎᑕᐅᔪᓐᓇᖅᑦᑕᕋᑦᑕ ᑎᒍᔭᐅᓯᒪᕙᒻᒥ ᓴᓇᖕᒍᐊᑎᑕᐅᔪᓐᓇᖅᑦᑕᕋᑦᑕ.

opportunity to carve in Fenbrook. My carving abilities also extend to carving animal bones, like blue whale bone, but soapstone is my favorite material. I really miss going to the sites where the soapstones are and digging out several hundred pounds of good quality soapstone. I use the traditional Inuit method for picking what I am going to carve. First I start by looking at the soapstone and thinking about the shape of the stone, and once I have decided what it looks like, I start the carving. I carve for myself because it makes me happy. I have a brother who also is a carver. I feel that carving is a tradition that will never die out. I am very thankful that I have the chance to carve while I am in Fenbrook.

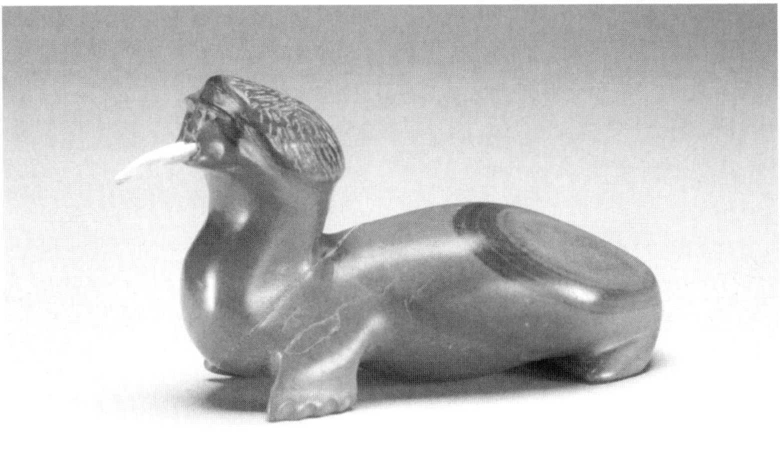

Shaman/Walrus with inset tusks, mottled green soapstone, 6.5"- 16.5 cm

ᐊᖕᒐᑯᖅ/ᐊᐃᕕᖅ ᑐᒑᓂᒃ, ᑐᖕᒍᔪᕈᔪᑐᖅ ᐅᒃᑯᓯᔅᓴᖅ

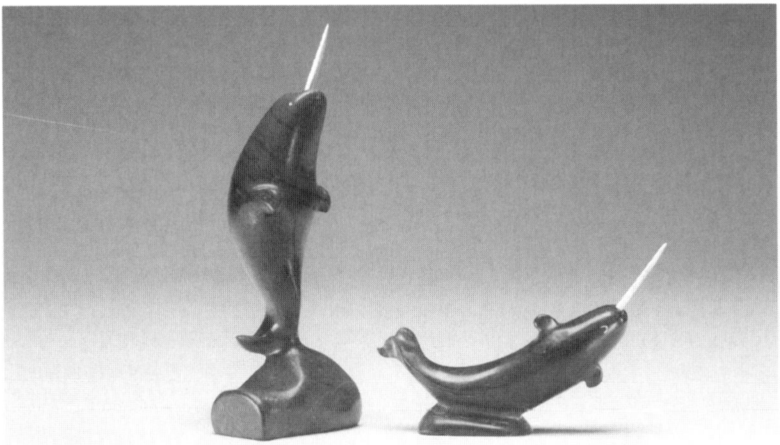

Narwhal with an inset antler tusk, together with a similar sculpture,

dark grey soapstone, 7"- 17.8 cm

ᖅᑭᓚᓗᒐᐅᑉ ᑐᒑᓂᒃ, ᐊᑕᖕᒥᖅᑐᑎᒃ ᐊᔾᔨᖕᒥᑦᑐᑦ ᓴᓇᖕᒍᐊᒐᓴᐃᑦ, ᐃᓱᐊᖕᒐᔪᑦ

ᐅᒃᑯᓯᔅᓴᐃᑦ

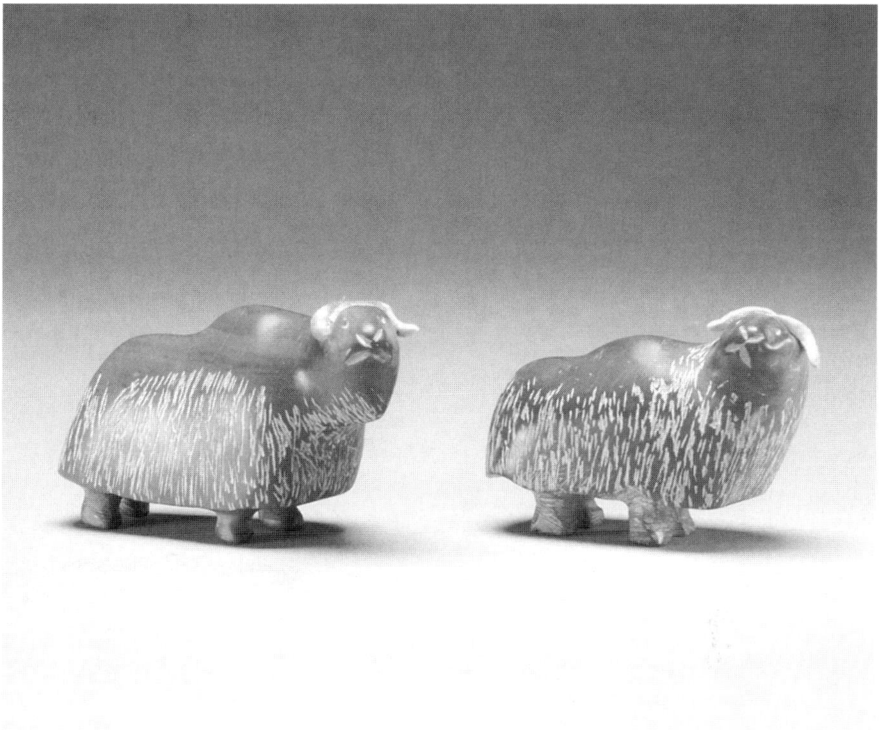

Musk Ox with bone horns together with a similar sculpture,

green soapstone, 4"- 10.2 cm

ᐅᒥᒻᒪᒃ ᓇᔾᔪᓕᒃ, ᐊᑕᖏᕐᑐᑎᒃ ᐊᔾᔨᒋᐸᓗᓐᓂᒃ ᓴᓇᖑᐊᒐᓴᐅᔪᑦ,

ᑐᖑᔪᕈᔪᑐᖅ ᐅᒃᑯᓯᔅᓴᖅ

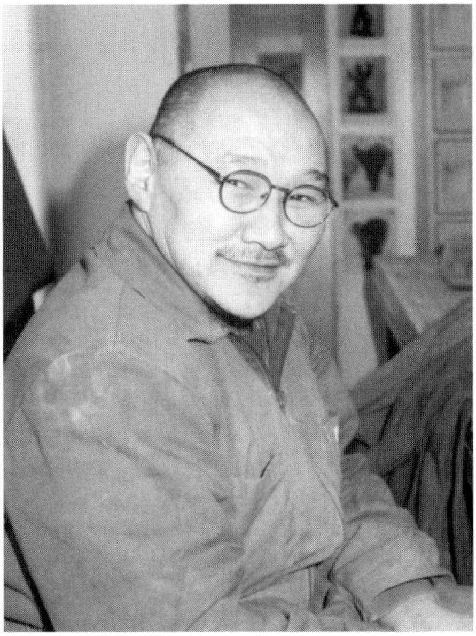

ᓴᓚ ᓂᕕᐊᕐᓯ

ᐃᓄᓚᐅᓯᒪᔪᖓ ᐃᓄᔾᔪᐊᖅᒥ ᓄᓇᕕᒻᒥ, 1965-ᖑᑎᓪᓗᖑ. ᓴᓇᖑᐊᑎᐅᓕᕐᑐᖓ ᐊᕐᕋᒍᓂᒃ 8 ᐅᕝᕙᓗ 10-ᓂᒃ. ᐱᕈᐸᓕᐊᑎᓪᓗᖓ ᓴᓇᖑᐊᓂᕐᒧᑦ ᓵᖕᒐᓗᐊᓚᐅᖕᒋᑦᑐᖓ. ᐱᖃᑎᒃᑲ ᐊᐃᐸᕆᓂᓴᕆᖃᑦᑕᓚᐅᕋᒃᑭᑦ ᖁᕕᐊᓱᖃᑎᒋᓪᓗᒋᑦ. ᐃᖅᑲᐅᒪᔪᖓ ᓯᕗᓪᓕᕐᐹᒥ ᓴᓇᖑᐊᕐᑐᖓ. 9-ᓂᒃ ᐊᕋᒍᖃᑦᑐᖓ. ᓇᑎᖑᐊᕐᒥᒃ ᐅᑯᓯᓴᒥᒃ ᓴᓇᖑᐊᓚᐅᓯᒪᔪᖓ. ᓴᓇᖑᐊᑎᐅᔪᔪᖓ 14-ᓄᑦ ᐊᕋᒍᒃᑲ ᑎᑭᑦᑐᒋᑦ ᓄᖅᑲᑕᖅᑯᖓ. ᐱᒋᐊᑲᓂᑕᐃᓐᓇᔪᔪᖓ ᑎᒍᔭᐅᓯᒪᕕᒻᒥᓕᕐᑐᖓ ᑕᕝᕙᓂ. ᖁᕕᐊᒋᔭᕋ ᓴᓇᖑᐊᕆᐊᓴᖅ ᐅᑯᓯᓴᒥᒃ ᐊᒻᒪᓗ ᑐᑦᑑᑉ ᓇᔪᖏᓐᓂᒃ ᑭᓯᐊᓂ ᖁᕕᐊᒋᓂᓴᕋ ᐅᑯᓯᓴᖅ ᓴᓇᖑᐊᕆᐊᖕᒐ. ᓴᓇᖑᐊᑕᒃᑲ ᐅᓂᑲᒥᖕᒐᓯᒪᒐᔫᓯᑦ ᐊᒻᒪᓗ ᐅᓂᑳᕐᑐᐊᒥᒃ ᐃᖅᑲᐅᒪᔭᒃᑲ ᓱᕈᓯᐅᓪᓗᖓ. ᐆᑦᑐᕆᓗᒍ ᐅᓂᒃᑳᒃᑐᐊᖅ ᐅᓂᑳᖕᒍᓯᒪᔭᖅ ᓴᓇᖑᐊᓯᒪᔭᕋ, ᕿᓚᓗᒐᖕᒍᐊᖅ ᐃᓅᑉ ᓇᐅᓕᓯᒪᖕᒍᐊᕐᑕᖓ ᓇᐅᓕᒻᒧᑦ. ᐃᓛᓐᓂᒃᑯᑦ ᐃᒻᒥᓂᒃ ᐅᓂᒃᑲᓕᐅᓱᕋ ᓴᓇᖑᐊᕐᑕᕋ ᐅᒪᔪᖑᐊᓄᑦ ᐅᕝᕙᓗ ᐃᓄᖑᐊᓄᑦ ᐅᓂᒃᑲᓕᐅᕐᑐᒍ. ᓴᓇᖑᐊᕐᓂᖅ ᐃᑲᔪᓂᓕᐊᓗᒃ ᐱᓐᓇᓱᓕᑎᑎᑲᓐᓂᐸᑦᑐᓂᓗ ᐃᓱᒪᒃᑯᑦ. ᐅᕙᓐᓄᑦ ᓴᓇᖑᐊᐸᑦᑐᖓ ᖁᕕᐊᓱᓕᑎᑎᕙᒻᒪᑦ ᐅᕙᓐᓂᒃ.

SALA NIVIAXIE

I was born in Inukjuak, Northern Quebec, in 1965. I have been carving soapstone for eight to ten years. When I was growing up, I wasn't really into soapstone carving. I spent my free time with my friends having fun. I remember my first carving experience. It was when I was nine years old. I carved a seal out of soapstone. I carved until I was about 14 and then I stopped. I finally started to carve again here at Fenbrook. I like to carve soapstone and a little bit of caribou antler, but mostly soapstone. My carvings are usually about stories and folktales that I remember from when I was a child. An example of a folktale that I have used for carving inspiration is about a whale that dragged a human with a harpoon. Sometimes I make a story and then I make carvings from the animals or people in the story. The carving is helpful because it stops me from getting stressed out and makes me more open-minded. I carve for myself, because it makes me happy. I also like to help the younger carvers when they are learning how to carve. Many of the men in my group like my carvings because they are funny. The dancing bears make them laugh. I like it that the carvings will bring my stories to others. When I leave Fenbrook Institution, I plan to continue carving, because I am very proud to be a creative soapstone carver. I would like to some day become a famous carver. I really enjoy the carvings that I make, and I believe my carvings will improve as I continue to develop my skills.

ᐃᑲᔪᕈᒪᓪᓗᖕᒐᓗ ᓄᑲᖅᑎᐅᓂᖅᓴᓂᒃ ᓴᓇᖕᒍᐊᓇᐅᐸᓕᐊᔪᓂᒃ. ᐊᒥᓱᑦ ᓴᓇᖕᒍᐊᖅᑲᑎᒋᕙᑦᑕᒃᑲ ᐊᖕᒍᑏᑦ ᐱᐅᓴᐸᑦᑐᑦ ᐅᕙᖕᒐ ᓴᓇᖕᒍᐊᒐᖕᒋᓐᓂᒃ ᐅᐱᓐᓇᖁᓂ ᖅᑯᖕᒐᓐᓇᖕᒐᑕ. ᓇᓄᖕᒍᐊᓕᐊᒃᑲ ᐃᓪᓚᕈᑕᐅᕙᑦᑐᑦ. ᑕᐃᒫᓗ ᖅᑯᕕᐊᓯᓪᓗᒍ ᓴᓇᖕᒍᐊᓂᒃᑯᑦ ᓴᖅᑭᐸᒻᒪᑦ ᐅᓂᑲᑕᒃᑲ ᐊᓯᓐᓄᑦ. ᑕᑉᐸᖕᒐᑦ ᐊᐅᓪᓚᕈᒪ ᑎᒍᔭᐅᓯᒪᕕᒻᒥᒃ, ᐸᖅᓇᑐᖕᒐ ᓴᓇᖕᒍᐊᖅᑲᑦᑖᓚᖃᒪ, ᐅᐱᒋᒐᒃᑯ ᖃᓄᕈᓗᔭᖅ ᓴᓇᖕᒍᐊᓇᐊᓴᖅ. ᖃᖕᒐᑐᐃᓐᓇᖅ ᓴᓇᖕᒍᐊᓱᖕᒍᓂᓐᓄᑦ ᖃᐅᔨᒪᔭᐅᓕᓛᕈᒪᔪᖕᒐ. ᖅᑯᕕᐊᒋᒐᑭᓪᓗ ᓴᓇᖕᒍᐊᐸᑦᑕᒃᑲ, ᐊᒻᒪᓗ ᐅᑉᐱᕈᓱᑲᒪ ᓴᓇᖕᒍᐊᓇᐅᐸᓕᐊᑐᐃᓇᖅᓂᐊᖃᒪ ᓴᓇᖕᒍᐊᑐᐃᓇᖅᑲᑦᑕᖅᓗᖕᒐ.

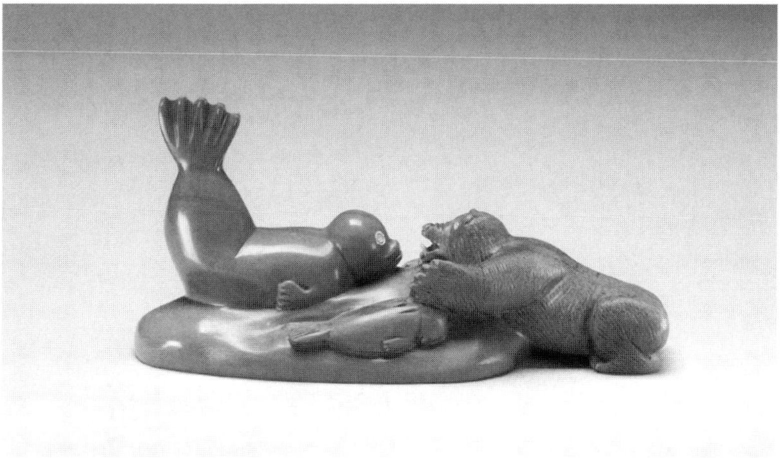

Polar Bear attacking a Seal, green soapstone, 7"- 17.8 cm

ᓇᓄᖅ ᐃᑕᒪᓵᓇᔪᖅ ᓇᑦᑎᕐᒥᒃ, ᑐᖕᒍᔪᕈᔪᑐᖅ ᐅᒃᑯᓯᔅᓴᖅ

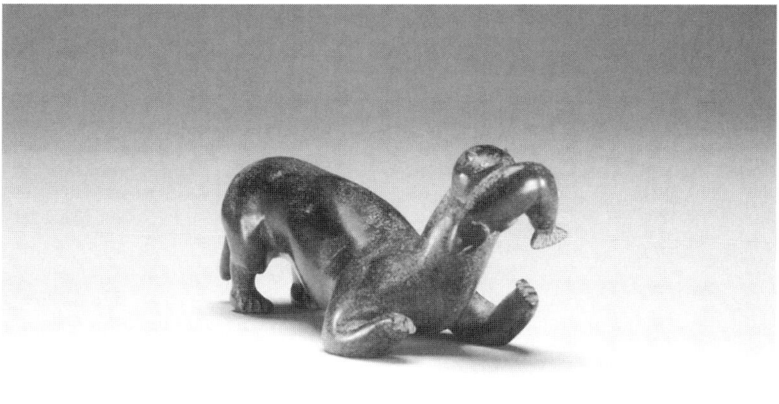

Otter having just caught a Fish, mottled dark soapstone 6"- 15.2 cm

ᐅᒪᔪᖅ ᓂᕆᔪᖅ ᐃᖃᓗᒻᒥᒃ, ᕿᓐᓈᖕᒐᔪᖅ ᐅᒃᑯᓯᔅᓴᖅ

Hᐊᒻ ᖃᐅᓐᓇᖅ

ᐃᓄᓚᐅᖅᓯᒪᔪᖓ ᓄᕕᐱᕆ 7, 1937-ᒥ ᓄᓇᓕᕐᕋᓛᕐᒥ ᐃᓪᓗᓕᐅᑉ ᖃᓂᒋᔭᓂ ᐊᑎᖃᕐᑐᖅ ᐃᖃᓗᐃᑦ. ᐅᐊᑎᐊᕈᑲᓪᓚᐅᓕᖓᑦ ᐃᓚᒋᑎᒍᑦ ᓄᑦᑎᓚᐅᓯᒪᔪᒍᑦ ᐃᑉᐱᐊᕐᔪᒻᒧᑦ. ᑕᐃᑲᓂ ᓄᓇᖃᓕᓚᐅᓯᒪᔪᒍᑦ ᐊᕐᕋᒍᓂᒃ ᐱᖓᓱᓂᒃ ᐃᓪᓗᓕᒻᒧᑦ ᓄᓇᖃᓕᓚᐅᕋᑕ. ᐃᓄᓱᑦᑑᓗᖓ ᐃᓕᐸᓕᐊᓕᓚᐅᕐᑐᖓ ᖃᓄᖅ ᐃᓄᐃᑦ ᐱᔾᔭᐃᓯᒪᓱᖑᒪᖓᑕ. ᐊᑖᑕᓐᓂᒃ ᓄᐊ ᐱᐅᒐᑐᕐᒥᒃ ᐃᓕᓂᐊᓚᐅᕐᑐᖓ ᖃᓄᖅ ᐊᖑᓇᓱᓐᓂᕐᒥᒃ. ᐃᓕᓐᓂᐊᑎᑕᐅᓪᓗᖓᓗ ᐃᓄᐃᑦ ᐱᖅᑯᓯᑐᖃᖏᑎᑐᑦ ᐃᓄᒐᓱᐊᕐᓂᕐᒥᒃ ᐊᒻᒪᓗ ᐃᖅᑲᓱᖃᑦᑕᕆᐊᖃᓐᓂᕐᒥᒃ ᐊᓯᓐᓄᑦ. ᓯᓇᓂᐊᓂᕐᒥᓪᓗ ᐃᓪᓗᓕᕐᐸᓯᐅᑉ ᖃᓂᒋᔮᓂ. ᓄᓇᓕᓐᓂ ᓄᓇᖃᑦᑐᑕ ᓴᓇᖑᐊᖃᑦᑕᔪᖏᑦᑐᖓ ᐅᑯᓯᓴᔭᓂᒃ ᑭᓯᐊᓂ ᑐᒫᓂᒃ ᓇᐅᓚᓕᐅᕐᐸᑦᑐᖓ ᐊᒻᒪᓗ ᓇᔾᔪᓂᒃ ᐊᖑᓇᓱᒍᑎᓴᓂᒃ. ᖃᐅᔨᒪᓕᕐᑐᖓ ᖃᓄᖅ ᓴᓇᖑᐊᑕᐅᓱᖑᒫᖓᑕ ᓇᔪᐃᑦ ᐊᒻᒪᓗ ᑐᒫᑦ ᖃᓄᕐᓗ ᓇᐅᓚᓕᐅᑕᐅᓱᖑᒻᒫᖓᑕ, ᐊᒻᒪᓗ ᓂᐅᕈᑎᒋᐸᑦᑐᒋᑦ. ᓴᓇᖑᐊᑎᕈᓚᐅᓇᖓ, ᐃᖅᑲᓇᐃᔭᕐᓯᒪᔪᖓ ᑯᐊᐸᖏᑦ ᓂᐅᕕᕕᖓᓄᑦ ᐅᔭᕿᐊᑎᐅᓗᖓ ᖃᓂᒋᔭᖓᓂ, ᐃᓪᓗᓕᐅᑉ ᑯᐊᐸᑯᓐᓄᑦ ᑐᕌᑐᓂᒃ. ᑕᐃᓱᒪᓂ ᐃᓱᒪᓗᐊᐸᓚᐅᖏᑦᑐᖓ ᓴᓇᖑᐊᓂᒐᓚᐅᑉ ᒥᔅᓵᓄᑦ, ᑭᓯᐊᓂ ᐃᓚᒃᑲ ᐃᓱᒪᒋᓂᕐᓴᓇᖃᑦᑕᔪᒐᒃᑭᑦ ᓂᕿᓴᓯᐅᖓᓇᐊᖏᑕ ᐊᓯᕙᕐᓂᒃᑯᑦ.

ᐊᕐᕋᒍ 2000-ᐅᓕᕐᑎᓪᓗᒍ ᓴᓇᖑᐊᕈᒪᕙᓕᐊᓕᓚᐅᕐᑐᖓ ᐅᑯᓯᓴᒥᒃ. ᐊᕐᕋᒎᒃ ᒪᕐᕉᓂᒃ, ᐃᓄᐃᑦ ᓴᓇᖑᐊᕐᑏᑦ ᐃᓕᓐᓂᐊᑎᑎᕙᓕᐊᓕᓚᐅᕐᑐᑦ ᐅᕙᓐᓂᒃ ᑕᐃᒪᖓᓂᑦᑐ ᐱᐅᓯᕙᓕᐊᖏᓐᓇᓕᕐᑐᑎᒃ. ᖃᐅᑕᒫᓗ ᓴᓇᖑᐊᖃᑦᑕᓕᕐᑐᖓ, ᐊᒥᓱᑲᓪᓚᓂᒃ ᓴᓇᖑᐊᓯᒪᓕᖅᑐᖓ. ᓴᓇᖑᐊᕆᐊᖓᓗ ᐱᐅᒥᓛᕆᓪᓗᖑ ᐅᑯᓯᔅᓴᖅ, ᓱᓕ ᐃᓛᓐᓂᒃᑯᑦ ᓴᐅᓂᕐᒥᒃ ᐅᕝᕙᓗ ᑑᒐᕐᒥᒃ ᐊᑐᕐᐸᑲᓗᐊᕐᑐᖓ ᐊᑐᓇᐊᖃᕋᐃᒐᒪ ᓰᕐᓗ ᐊᐃᕕᖑᐊᓕᐅᕈᒪ. ᐊᒻᒪᓗ ᓴᓇᖑᐊᕈᓯᕋ ᐊᔾᔨᐅᖏᑦᑐᖅ. ᓴᓇᖑᐊᑕᒃᑲ ᐃᔾᔪᐊᓯᖃᑦᑕᕐᑐᑦ ᐃᓄᐃᑦ ᐱᖅᑯᓯᑐᖃᖓᓂᒃ ᐊᒻᒪᓗ ᐃᓕᕐᑯᓯᑐᖃᖓᓂᒃ ᑲᔪᓯᐅᑎᓚᖓᔭᕋ ᓴᓇᖑᐊᕐᓂᖅ ᐅᒃᑯᓯᔅᓯᒥᒃ, ᐊᒻᒪᓗ ᐃᓄᓯᖃᐃᓇᓂᐊᕐᑐᖓ ᐃᓄᐃᑦ ᐃᓕᕐᑯᓯᑐᖃᖓᓂᒃ. ᓴᓇᖑᐊᖏᓐᓇᖃᑦᑕᓂᐊᕐᑐᖓᓗ ᐱᕕᖃᕐᓂᓕᒫᓐᓂ ᐃᓄᒐᓱᐊᕈᑎᒋᓯᓐᓈᓪᓗ. ᐃᓄᐃᓪᓗ ᐱᖅᑯᓯᖓ ᓱᓕᓂᒃᑯ ᑕᑯᓴᐅᑎᓐᓇᕋᓱᓪᓗᒍ. ᑕᑯᓐᓇᓚᐅᕐᑐᒍᓗ ᐅᑯᓯᔅᓴᖅ ᑭᓱᓂᐊᕐᒫᖓᖅ, ᑕᑯᓐᓇᖑᐊᕐᐸᓕᐊᓗᒍ ᖃᓄᖅ ᓴᓇᖑᐊᓂᐊᕐᒫᖓᒃᑯ, ᒪᓕᑦᑐᒍ

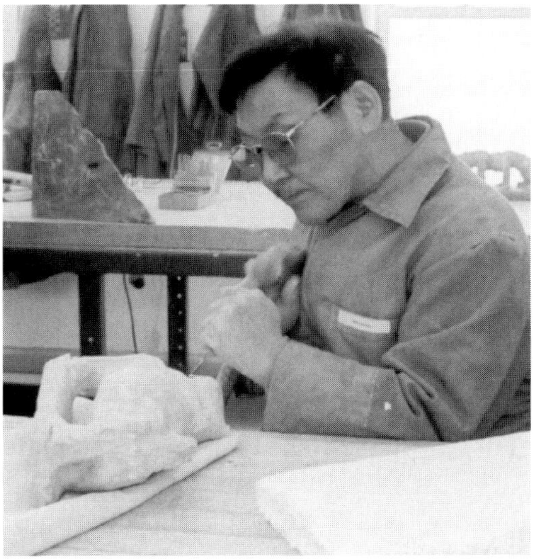

HAM QAUNAQ

I was born on the 7th of November, 1937 in a small outpost camp at Iqaluit, near Igloolik, Nunavut. Later my family moved into Ipiaqjuk, Arctic Bay, and we lived within that community for three years before returning to Igloolik. Throughout my younger years, I learned the skills of Inuit tradition for survival. I learned how to hunt from my father, Noah Piugartuk, and I was taught how to work and share together in everyday life around the coastlines of the Igloolik area. When I lived in the community I did not carve soapstone carvings but I carved ivory and antler to make materials for hunting. I knew how to carve the antler and ivory to make harpoons, and I sold them. Before I was a carver, I also worked for the local co-operative store to harvest soapstone near the Igloolik area for the co-op's soapstone supply. At the time, it did not interest me to create soapstone sculptures, and instead I concentrated on supporting my family by hunting wild animals in the countryside of the Northwest of Baffin Island.

ᖃᓄᐃᑦᑐᓂᖓ ᐅᑯᓯᓴᐅᖅ. ᓴᓇᑎᑕᐅᖃᑦᑕᓯᒪᒥᔪᒍᑦ ᑐᓯᕋᑕᐅᔪᓂᒃ ᐊᔾᔨᒋᖏᑦᑐᓂᒃ ᓲᕐᓗ ᐃᓄᓱᖑᐊᓂᒃ, ᑭᓯᐊᓂᓕ ᖁᕕᐊᒋᓂᖅᓴᕋ ᐅᕙᓐᓂᒃ ᐃᓱᒪᓕᐊᕆᓗᒍ ᐊᒻᒪᓗ ᐊᖏᔪᑎᓂᒃ ᓴᓇᖑᐊᕆᐊᓴᖅ. ᐃᓛᓐᓂᑯᓪᓗ ᓴᓇᖑᐊᐸᑦᑐᖓ ᐊᖓᑯᖑᐊᓂᒃ, ᐊᖓᑯᐃᑦ ᒥᔅᓴᓄᑦ ᐊᑖᑕᒪ ᐅᓂᑲᐅᑎᕙᓚᐅᖅᓯᒪᒻᒫᖓ. ᐊᖓᑯᐃᑦ ᓴᖏᔪᓪᓚᕆᐊᓗᓂᖓᑕ ᐱᔪᓐᓇᓂᓕᐊᓗᓗᑎᓪᓗ ᐅᓂᑳᖅ ᑐᓴᐅᒪᔭᒃᑲ ᒥᔅᓴᓄᑦ ᓴᓇᖑᐊᓂᒃᑯᑦ ᓴᓇᕙᑦᑕᒃᑲ. ᐃᓚᖏᑦ ᐊᖓᑯᐃᑦ ᐱᐅᔪᑦ ᐃᓚᖏᓪᓗ ᐱᐅᕙᓐᓂᖏᒻᒥᔪᑦ. ᑭᓇᐅᔭᓕᐅᕋᓱᓐᓂᒃᑯᑦ ᐊᑭᑐᕋᐅᑎᔪᖃᑦᑎᓪᓗᒍ ᓴᓇᖑᐊᓯᒪᓚᐅᕐᑐᖓ ᐊᖓᑯᖑᐊᒥᒃ. ᑖᓐᓇ ᓴᓇᖑᐊᓯᒪᔭᕋ ᐊᖓᑯᖑᐊᖅ ᖁᑉᐹ ᕿᓚᓗᒐᖑᐊᖑᓪᓗᓂ ᐊᒻᒪᓗ ᖁᐸᑲᓂᐊ ᓇᓄᖑᐊᖑᓪᓗᓂ ᖃᓄᐃᑐᑐᐃᓐᓇᐅᔭᓐᓇᖓᑕ ᐃᒪᕐᒥᐅᑕᐃᑦ, ᒪᓕᑦᑎᓱᖑᒥᒪᑕ ᐃᓄᐃᓐᓂᒃ ᐃᓚᖏᑦ ᑕᐃᒫᒃ ᔭᒐᓕᖅᑭᓱᖑᕗᑦ.

In the year 2000, I became interested in doing artwork with soapstone. For the past couple of years, the Inuit carving instructors have helped me in my carving and my carvings have improved. I now carve every day, and I have made a lot of carvings. My favorite material is soapstone, but sometimes I use a bit of bone or ivory to carve tusks for my walrus sculpture. I think that I have used original art forms and that I have unique style. My carvings imitate the past traditions and culture of the Inuit. I will continue to make soapstone carving my hobby and living at the same time, and so will continue to live in the true Inuit traditions. I decide what carving I am going to make by looking at the soapstone. I picture what I am going to make, based on what kind of shape the stone has. I have in the past made commissioned pieces like Inukshuks and others, but I prefer to decide my own subjects. I enjoy carving and I like to make large carvings and use my own ideas. Sometimes I carve Shamans. I know about shamans from stories that my father used to tell me. I use the shaman stories in my carvings because shamans are very strong and powerful. In the Inuit tradition some shamans were good and some were bad. For the Inside Out Charity Auction, I worked on a caving of a Shaman. The Shaman is half beluga and half polar bear, and used to live underwater and could transform into all kinds of animals, trapping people by letting them follow him until the people would get lost.

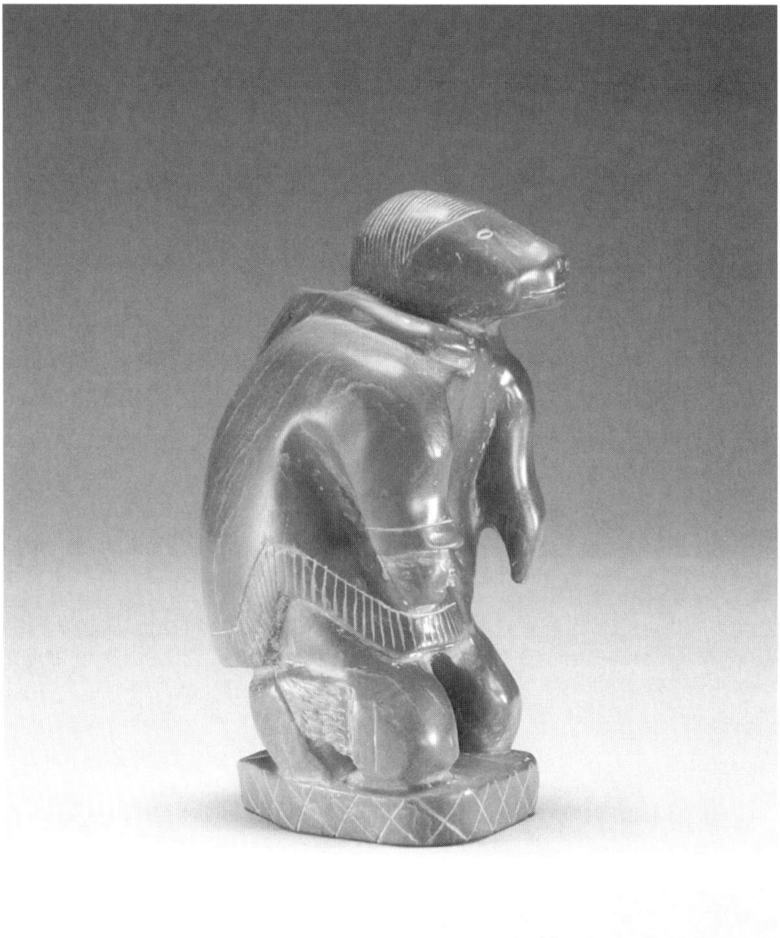

Transformation sculpture of a Shaman/Polar Bear, marbled green soapstone, 7"- 17.8 cm

ᐊᖕᒐᒃᑯᖅ ᓴᓇᖕᒍᐊᒐᔅᓴᕈᑦᑐᖅ/ᓇᓄᖅ, ᑐᖕᒍᔪᕈᔪᑦᑐᑦᓗᓂ ᓴᓇᖕᒍᐊᒐᔅᓴᖅ

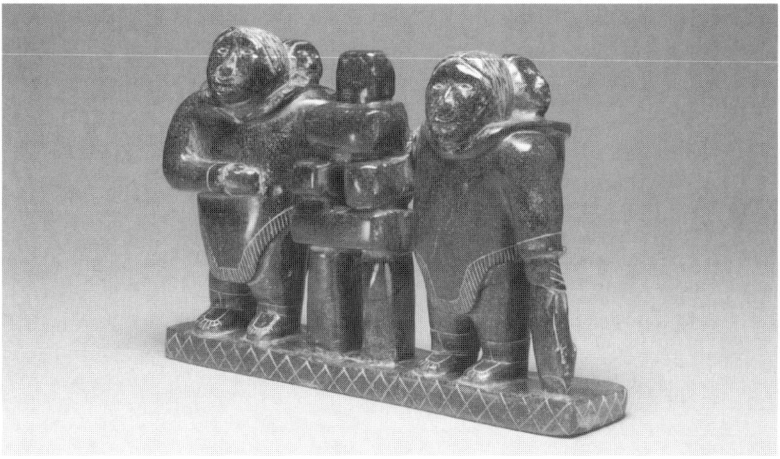

Two Inuit women carrying children in their amoutis and standing beside an Inukshuk, dark soapstone, 13"- 33 cm

ᒪᕐᕉᒃ ᐊᕐᓇᓗᑳᒃ ᐃᓅᒃ ᐊᒪᕐᑑᒃ ᓱᕈᓯᕐᒥᒃ ᓇᖏᕐᑐᑎᒃ ᐃᓄᒃᓲᑉ ᓴᓂᐊᓂ,
ᕿᕐᓈᖕᒐᔪᖅ ᐅᒃᑯᓯᒃᓴᖅ

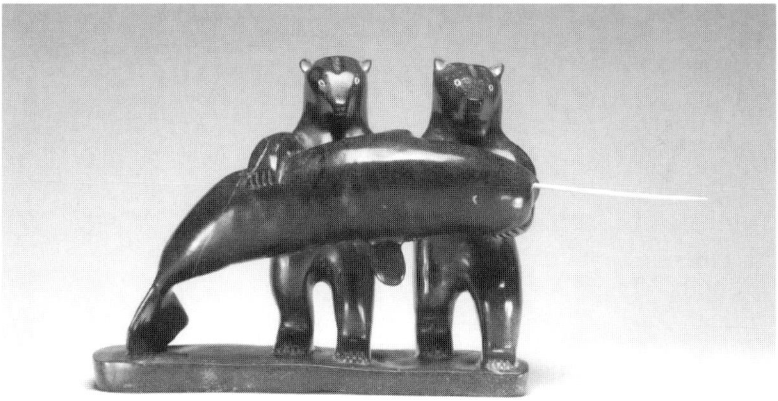

Two Polar Bears holding a Narwhal with inset antler tusk,
dark soapstone, 20"- 50.8 cm

ᒪᕐᕉᒃ ᓇᓄᒃ ᑎᒍᒥᐋᕐᑑᒃ ᑐᒐᕐᒥᒃ ᕿᓚᓗᒐᕐᔪᑦ, ᕿᓐᓇᖕᒐᔪᖅ ᐅᒃᑯᓯᒃᓴᖅ

ᐃᑎᒐᖅᑕᑖᖅ ᔭᐃᒥᓯ ᕋᐃᒋ

ᐃᓅᓚᐅᖅᓯᒪᔪᖓ ᑭᙵᐃᑦ ᓯᓚᑖᓂ ᐅᖓᓯᓐᓂᖅᑲᑦᑐᖅ 75-ᒪᐃᓕᒥᒃ,ᐊᑎᓕᒃ ᓄᕗᔾᔪᐊᒥᒃ. ᐊᑖᑕᓯᐊᕐᒪ ᓄᓇᒥᓂᖓ ᓄᓇᓕᕌᓚᓂ. ᓴᓇᖑᐊᕐᑎᐅᓕᕐᑐᖓ ᐊᕐᕋᒍᐃᑦ ᐊᕙᑏᑦ ᐅᖓᑖᓂᒐᓚᒃ. ᖁᕕᐊᒋᔭᕋ ᓴᓇᖑᐊᖢᐊᓴᖅ ᐅᒃᑯᓯᔅᓴᓂᒃ, ᓯᕗᓪᓕᖅᐹᒥ ᓴᓇᖑᐊᖢᐅᐸᓪᓕᐊᓪᓗᖓ ᑐᑦᑑᑉ ᓇᔾᔪᖏᒃ ᓴᓇᖑᐊᖢᐅᓴᕈᑎᒋᓯᒪᔭᒃᑲ. ᓱᓕᓕ ᑕᐅᑐᒍᓐᓃᓚᐅᕐᓇᖓ, ᐃᖅᑲᐅᒪᒻᒥᔪᖓ ᓴᓇᖑᐊᓚᐅᓯᒪᒐᒪ ᐅᑯᓯᔅᓴᔭᒥᒃ ᐊᐃᕕᒧᑦ ᓂᐊᖁᖑᐊᖑᓪᓗᓂ. ᑕᑯᓐᓈᐸᔪᒐᒪ ᐃᓚᒃᑲ ᓴᓇᖑᐊᑎᑦᑐᒋᑦ ᓴᓇᖑᐊᕐᑕᖏᓪᓗ ᒥᔅᓯᑕᐸᓪᓕᐊᓕᕋᐃᒻᒪᑕ. ᓄᓇᓕᕋᓚᒥᐅᑕᐅᓚᐅᓯᒪᔪᒍᑦ ᐊᕋᒍᖃᓕᕋᒪ 10 ᐅᕝᕙᓗ 11-ᓂᒃ ᐃᓚᒌᑎᒍᑦ ᑭᙵᕐᓄᑦ ᓅᑎᓚᐅᓯᒪᔪᒍᑦ. ᒐᕙᒪᒃᑯᑦ ᓅᑎᑎᕙᓪᓕᐊᓕᖅᑎᓪᓗᒋᑦ ᓄᓇᓕᓐᓄᑦ ᐃᓕᓐᓂᐊᖁᔨᓪᓗᑎᒃ ᐅᕙᑎᓐᓂᒃ ᐊᒻᒪᓗ ᐅᑭᐅᑕᑐᒧᑦ ᓴᖅᑭᐸᓕᐊᓕᕐᑎᓪᓗᒋᑦ ᐊᐅᓚᔾᔪᓯᖏᑦ. 19-ᓂᒃ ᐅᑭᐅᖃᓕᕐᑐᖓ ᑕᐅᑐᒍᓐᓂᓚᐅᓯᒪᔪᖓ ᐱᓂᕐᓗᐊᕿᓪᓗᖓ. 20-ᕈᔭᖏᓐᓂᓕᕐᑐᖓ ᓴᓇᖑᐊᖢᐅᓴᐸᓪᓕᐊᓕᓚᐅᕐᑐᖓ ᒥᑭᔪᑎᓂᒃ ᐅᑯᓯᔅᓴᓂᒃ. ᓯᕗᓪᓕᖅᐹᒥ ᐱᒡᒐᓇᓚᖅᐅᓯᒪᔪᖅ ᐃᓗᑦᑏᒋᐊᓴᖅ ᐅᑯᓯᓴᒥᒃ, ᑭᓯᐊᓂ ᐱᒋᐅᐸᓕᐊᖏᓐᓇᓚᐅᕐᑐᖓ ᓴᓇᖑᐊᖏᓐᓇᓕᕋᒪ ᐱᐅᓯᕙᓪᓕᐊᖏᓐᓇᕐᑐᑎᓪᓗ ᓴᓇᖑᐊᑕᒃᑲ. ᑕᑯᖃᑕᓐᓂᑯᒃᑲᓗ ᐃᖅᑲᐅᒪᒐᓱᐸᑦᑐᒋᑦ ᓱᓕ ᑕᐅᑐᓱᖓᕐᑐᖓ, ᐃᓱᒪᒃᑯᑦ ᑕᑯᓐᓇᖑᐊᕐᑕᕋ ᒪᓕᑉᐸᓕᐊᓪᓗᒍ. ᐃᓛᓐᓂᒃᑯᑦ ᐊᓯᕈᖅᓇᑲᐃᓐᓇᐸᑦᑐᖅ ᓴᓇᖑᐊᖅᑐᓂ ᑭᓕᖃᑕᓱᖓ, ᓴᓇᖑᐊᕈᑏᑦ ᐃᓚᖏᑦ ᐃᐱᑐᓂᖏᓐᓄᑦ, ᑭᓯᐊᓂ ᓄᖅᑲᑐᐃᓇᐸᖏᑦᑐᖅ ᑕᐃᒪᐃᑲᓗᐊᕐᑎᓪᓗᒍ. ᓴᓇᖑᐊᑕᒃᑲᓗ ᒥᓯᑖᕋᐃᒻᒪᑕ ᖁᕕᐊᓇᕐᓯᕙᓪᓕᐊᖏᓐᓇᐸᑦᑐᖅ ᓴᓇᖑᐊᕈᒪᓕᐸᓕᐊᑐᐃᓐᓇᖅᑐᖓ. ᖃᐅᔨᒃᑲᓂᕐᓯᒪᒐᒪᓗ ᖃᓄᖅ ᐊᒡᒐᑲ ᐊᑐᕈᓐᓇᕐᒪᖔᑭᑦ; ᐊᒡᒐᑲᓗ ᑐᑭᒧᐊᕈᑎᒋᕙᒃᑲᑭᑦ ᓴᓇᖑᐊᑕᓐᓄᑦ.

ᓴᓇᖑᐊᒐᑲᓗ ᑕᑯᓴᐅᕙᓕᐊᓕᕐᑐᑎᒃ ᑕᑯᔭᒐᖃᕐᕕᓂ ᑲᓇᑕᒥ, ᓴᓇᖑᐊᒐᓐᓂ ᓂᐅᕕᕐᑎᓄᑦ ᐱᐅᒥᔭᐅᕙᑦᑐᑎᒃ ᐊᒻᒪᓗ ᑭᒃᑯᑐᐃᓐᓇᕐᓄᑦ. ᓴᓇᖑᐊᒐᒃᑲ ᐊᑎᓕᐅᕐᓯᒪᕙᑦᑕᒃᑲ ᔭᐃᒻᔅ ᕋᐃᒥᓚᓯᒪᓗᑎᒃ ᐊᑖᓂ ᓴᓇᖑᐊᒐᒻᒪ. ᖃᖓᑐᐃᓐᓇᖅ ᓯᕗᓕᕐᐹᖑᖃᑕᐅᔪᒪᔪᖓ ᐃᓕᓴᓇᔭᐅᓕᖓ ᑲᓇᑕᒥ ᓴᓇᖑᐊᖃᑦᑕᓂᓐᓄᑦ ᑕᐅᑐᖏᑑᓪᓗᖓ. ᐃᓱᒪᓱᓇᖏᑐᑰᕕᒻᒥᓱᖓ ᐱᕕᖃᓐᓂᓴᐅᓯᒪᕗᖓ ᓴᓇᖑᐊᓂᕐᒥᒃ, ᐊᒻᒪᓗ ᐃᑲᔫᑎᖃᕐᓯᒪᕗᖅ ᓴᓇᖑᐊᖢᐅᐹᓕᕐᓯᒪᒐᒪ ᐃᓛᓂᑯᓪᓗ ᖁᕕᐊᒋᓂᕐᐸᖢᕙᑦᑕᕋ ᓴᓇᖑᐊᕐᑕᒃᑲ ᐅᓂᑳᓕᐅᕐᐸᓕᐊᓪᓗᒋᑦ.

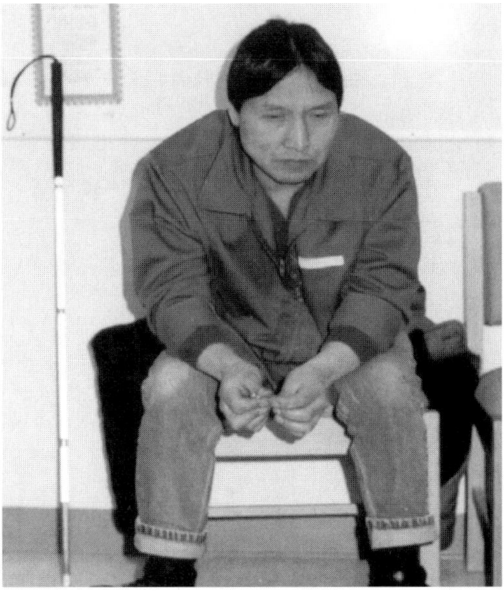

ETEEGAQTATAAQ JAMISIE RAGEE

I was born 75 miles northwest from Cape Dorset, in my grandfather's outpost camp at Nuvoutjuaq, Nunavut. I have been carving now for a little bit over 20 years. I like to carve soapstone, but when I first started to carve I used antlers as my practice material. Before I lost my sight, I can remember carving one little walrus head in soapstone. I would watch some of my family members shaping up small sculptures of serpentine soapstone. I lived on the land until I was about 10 or 11, after which I moved with my parents and other family members into the settlement of Cape Dorset, Baffin Island. The government posted the settlement for us to learn and adapt to a new modern society in the far north. At the age of 19 I lost my eyesight due to an accident. In my mid-twenties I started to practice and work on small soapstone carvings. At first, I found it difficult to shape up my carvings, but I noticed that the more that I carved, the better my carvings became. I taught myself by recalling some of the carvings

ᐆᑦᑐᑎᒋᓗᒍ, ᓴᓇᖕᒍᐊᓯᒪᔪᒐᒪ ᐊᐃᖓᖕᒍᐊᕐᒥᒃ ᖁᓕᑕᐅᔭᕐᓯᒪᖕᒍᐊᕐᑐᒥᒃ ᐊᕐᓇᓯᐅᒻᒥᒃ, ᐅᓂᒃᑳᕐᓯᒪᓪᓗᒍ ᐊᐃᖓᐅᑉ ᒥᔅᓵᓄᑦ. ᓇᓅᖅ ᐱᒋᐊᖅᑲᑦ ᐊᐃᖓᕐᒥᑦ, ᐊᐃᖓᕐᓗ ᑐᓛᕐᒥᓄᑦ ᑐᕐᑯᑎᓪᓗᓂ ᓇᓄᕐᒥᒃ ᐅᐊᑦᑎᐊᕈᓕᖕᒐᑦ ᑕᑯᓕᕐᑐᒥᓂᖅ ᐊᕐᓇᓗᑲᕐᒥᒃ ᓇᓄᖁᒥᒃ ᖁᓕᑕᐅᔭᕐᓯᒪᔪᒥᒃ. ᐅᓪᓗᒥᐅᓕᕐᑐᖅ ᐊᐃᙶᑦ ᐊᑐᕐᑐᔮᑎᓪᓗᒋᑦ ᓇᓄᖁᒥᒃ ᑕᑯᔭᐅᔪᓇᕐᓯᔪᑦ.

ᐅᐱᑯᓱᒃᑲᒪ ᐅᒃᑯᓯᓴᐃᑦ ᐃᐱᓇᕐᑐᖅᑲᓇᖕᒋᑕ, ᐅᐊᑎᐊᕈᑲᓪᓚᐅᓕᕐᑐᖅ ᓂᓪᓕᐊᖅᑎᖅᑲᓚᐅᓯᒪᒐᒪ ᓴᓇᖕᒍᐊᕐᑎᒥᒃ, ᐅᖅᑲᓚᐅᓯᒪᒻᒪᑦ ᐊᔨᖕᒋᒋᓐᓂᖕᒋᓐᓂ ᓴᓇᖕᒍᐊᕐᑏᑦ. ᐅᖅᑲᕐᑐᓂᓗ, ᓴᓇᖕᒍᐊᑎᐅᓕᕐᒥ ᐊᑯᓂᒃ ᐃᓕᓴᖅᓯᔪᓐᓇᕐᓯᔪᖅ ᓴᓇᖕᒍᐊᒐᐃᑦ ᐃᓚᖕᒋᑦ ᐃᐱᓇᕐᓂᖅᑲᓇᖕᒋᑕ. ᑕᐃᓱᒪᓂ ᑐᑭᓯᑎᐊᓚᐅᓯᒪᖕᒋᑦᑐᖕᒐ ᖅᑲᓄ ᑐᑭᖅᑲᓪᓚᓇᑲᓗᐊᕐᒪᖕᒑᖅ, ᒫᓐᓇᐅᓕᕐᑐᖅ ᑐᑭᓯᓕᕐᑐᖕᒐ. ᐊᑯᓂᑲᓪᓚᒃ ᓴᓇᖕᒍᐊᖅᑲᑦᑕᕐᓯᒪᓕᖁᒪ ᐅᐱᕈᓱᓕᕐᓯᒪᓕᕐᑐᖕᒐᑦᑕᐅᖅ ᐃᐱᓇᕐᓂᖅᑲᓇᖕᒋᑕ ᓴᓇᖕᒍᐊᒐᐃᑦ. ᐅᖅᑲᑲᓐᓂᕈᒪᕗᖕᒐ ᓴᓇᖕᒍᐊᕐᑎᓄᑦ ᓴᓇᖕᒍᐊᕐᓂᖅ ᐊᔅᓱᐊᓗᒃ ᐊᑐᑎᖅᑲᖕᒐᑦ ᖅᑲᓄᑐᐃᓐᓇᖅ ᓲᕐᓗ ᑕᕐᓂᒃᑯᑦ ᐊᒻᒪᓗ ᐃᐱᓂᐊᓂᒃᑯᑦ.

that were in my memory before I had lost my sight, copying from my memory. It is a challenge to carve, because the caving tools are sharp and I often cut my fingers while I worked, but that didn't stop me. I was encouraged by the fact that each time, the carvings turned out better. And I have learned to use my hands; they would feel and guide around the carvings.

My artworks have been exhibited in art galleries throughout Canada, and have been greatly admired by private collectors and by other art dealers. On each of my carvings, I sign under the name James Ragee. I hope one day to be one of the first blind people to be recognized among Canadian artists as a famous carver. My experience in Fenbrook has given me more time to carve, and as a result, it has helped my carving technique. The subjects that I like to deal with in my carvings can sometimes come out of stories that I make up. For example, I carved a walrus wearing a woman's parka and there is a story about the carving. It is about a walrus, that when a bear attacked her, turned around and struck the bear with her tusk and killed him. Later she saw a woman wearing a fashionable parka and decided to copy the woman and make a parka out of the bearskin. Today the walrus can be seen wearing the beautiful polar bear parka.

I believe that soapstone can have a spirit in it. Some years ago when I was talking with an experienced carver, he told me that there is a difference between each carving. He told me that, as an experienced carver, he could tell that some of the carvings had a spirit within them. At the time I didn't quite understand what he meant, but now I do. I have been carving so long that I feel that there are spirits in them. I also would suggest carving to anyone because it has turned out to be useful in a lot of ways, both spiritually and emotionally.

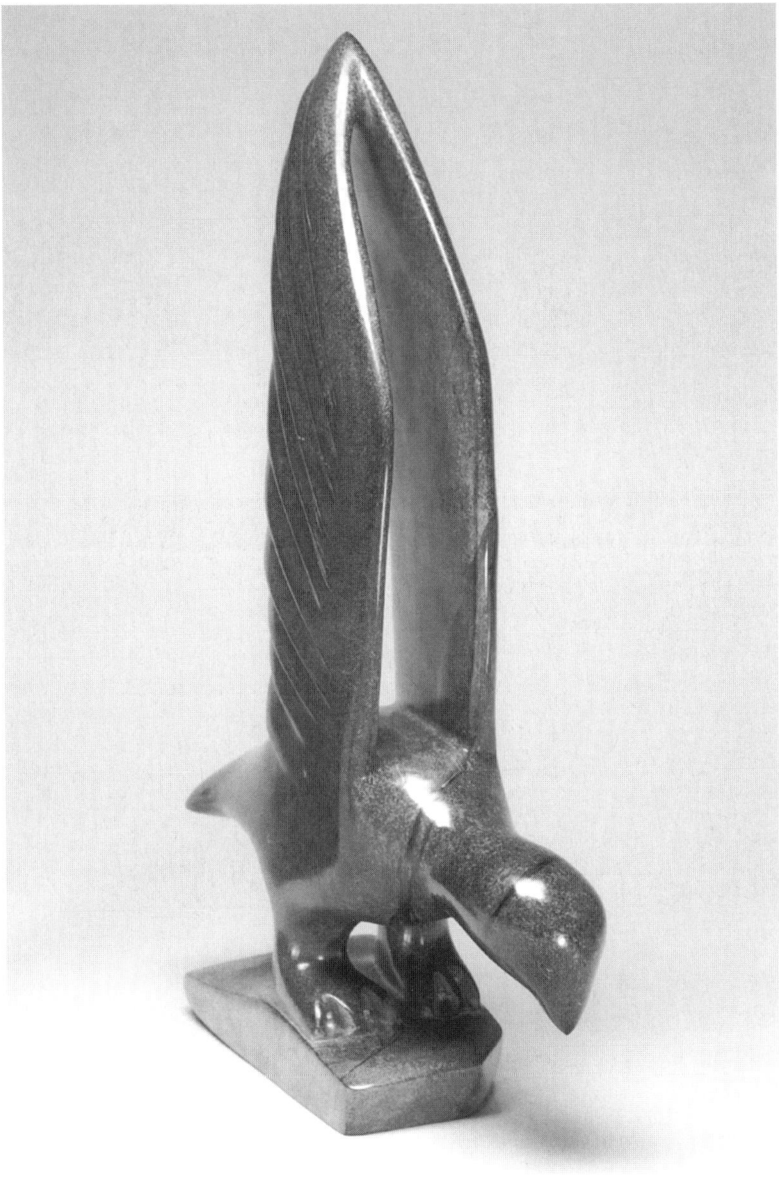

Bird with upswept wings, mottled dark grey soapstone, 18"- 45.7 cm

ᑎᒻᒥᐊᖅ ᐃᓴᕈᓕᒃ, ᐃᓱᐊᙵᕙᖅ ᐅᒃᑯᓯᒃᓴᖅ

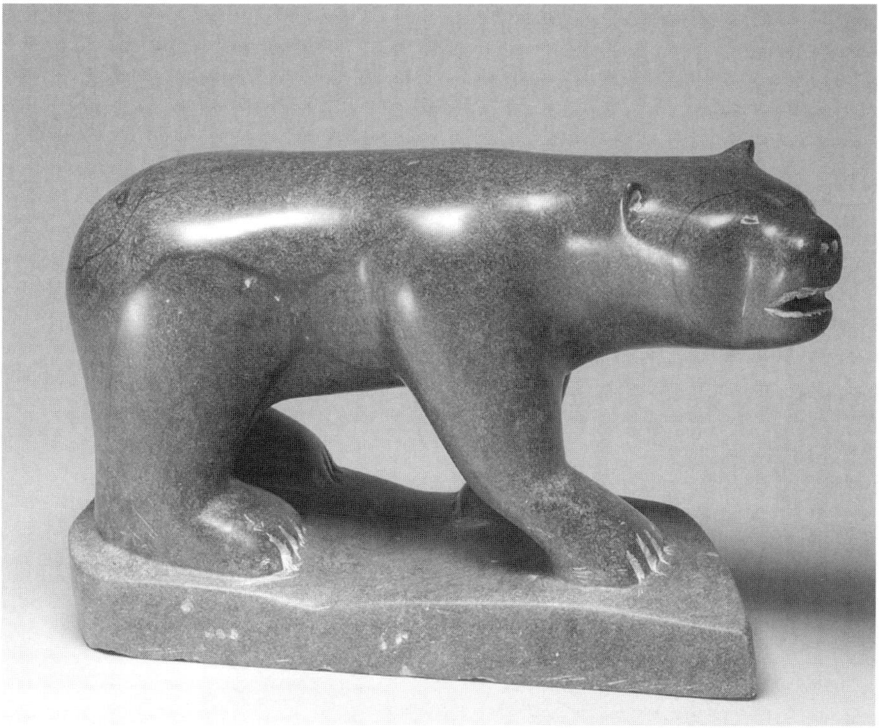

A walking Polar Bear, mottled dark grey soapstone, 12"- 30.5 cm

ᐱᓱᑦᑐᖅ ᓇᓄᖅ, ᐃᓱᐊᖕᒪᔪᖅ ᐅᒃᑯᓯᒃᓴᖅ

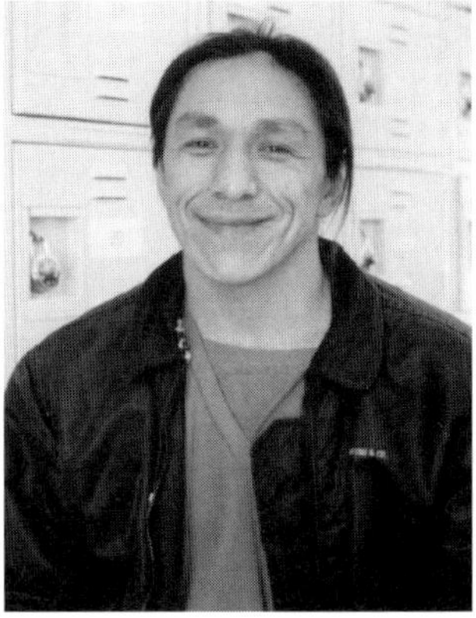

ᐊᓕᒃ ᓵᓚ

ᐃᓅᓚᐅᓯᒪᔪᖓ 1966-ᖑᑎᓪᓗᒍ ᓴᓂᑭᓗᐊᖅᒥ. ᓴᓇᖑᐊᓇᐅᕈᑎᒋᓚᐅᓯᒪᔭᕋ ᓇᑎᖑᐊᖅ ᒥᑭᔪᕈᓗᒃ 8-ᓂᒃ ᐊᕐᕋᒍᖃᑦᑐᖓ. ᓄᓇᖃᓚᐅᓯᒪᔪᖓ ᑯᐸᐃᐸᓯᒻᒥ 12-ᓂᒃ ᐊᕋᒍᖃᓕᖅᑎᓪᓗᖓ. ᐊᒻᒪᓗ ᐃᖅᑲᓇᐃᔮᕐᑕᕋᒪ ᐃᓄᕕᒥᓂᕐᓄᑦ ᓄᓕᓚᐅᓯᒪᔪᖓ ᓴᓂᑭᓗᐊᖅᒧᑦ. ᓴᓂᑭᓗᐊᕐᒥ ᐃᖅᑲᐅᒪᔪᖓ ᐊᒥᓱᑲᓪᓚᓗᐃᑦ ᓴᓇᖑᐊᖅᑲᑦᑕᓚᐅᓯᒪᒻᒪᑕ ᐃᓄᐃᑦ ᑕᐃᒪᑐᐊᕐᓗ ᐃᒻᒥᓂᒃ ᑭᓱᖃᑦᑎᐸᑦᑐᑎᒃ ᑭᓇᐅᔭᓕᐅᕈᑎᒋᓪᓗᒋᑦ. ᓄᑲᕋᓗ ᐊᑕᐅᑎᒃᑯᑦ ᐃᓕᓚᐅᓯᒪᔪᒍᒃ ᓴᓇᖑᐊᓂᒃᒥᒃ ᓴᓂᑭᓗᐊᒥ. ᑕᕝᕗᖓ ᑎᒍᔭᐅᓯᒪᕕᒻᒧᑦ ᑎᑭᑲᒪ ᓴᓇᖑᐊᕋᓯᑕᐅᑎᒋᔪᖏᑦᑐᖓ ᑕᕙᑕᐅᑎᒥᒃ. ᓴᓇᖑᐊᕋᓯᑕᓕᑕᐃᓐᓇᔪᔪᖓ ᓴᓇᖑᐊᒐᑲ ᑕᐃᒪᖓᓂᒃ ᐱᐅᓯᕙᓕᐊᖏᓐᓇᕐᓯᒪᔪᑦ. ᖁᕕᐊᒋᓛᕋ ᓴᓇᖑᐊᓇᐊᖓ ᐅᑯᓯᔅᓴᖅ. ᓴᓇᖑᐊᖅᑕᓯᒪᒐᓗᐊᕐᒥᔪᖓ ᔫᒐᕐᒥᒃ ᑭᓯᐊᓂ ᐅᑯᓯᔅᓴᖅ ᐊᑲᐅᒥᓂᖅᓴᕋ ᓴᓇᖑᐊᓇᐊᖓ. ᕿᒥᕉᖅᑲᓚᐅᕐᑐᒍ ᐅᑯᓯᓴᖅ ᐱᕆᐊᓕᑕᐃᓐᓇᐸᑦᑐᖓ. ᖃᓄᐃᓕᖓᓂᖓ ᒪᓕᑦᑐᒍ ᐅᑯᓯᓴᐅᑉ. ᑕᑯᓐᓇᖑᐊᕐᑐᕆᑦ ᐅᒪᔪᐃᑦ ᑕᑯᓚᐅᓯᒪᔭᒃᑲ ᓄᓇᒥ. ᖃᐅᔨᒪᓚᐅᓯᒪᖏᓐᓇᒪ ᖃᓄᖅ ᐱᔭᓇᑕᐅᓚᓇᓱᖑᒻᒪᖖᒐᑕ, ᑭᓯᐊᓂᓕ ᐃᓕᐹᓕᕐᓯᒪᓕᕐᑐᖓ ᑐᐊᕕᐊᓇᖕᒋᓪᓗᒍ. ᓄᓇᑎᓐᓂ ᐊᓯᕙᓂᓴᐅᕙᓚᐅᕋᒪ, ᓴᓇᖑᐊᓂᖅ ᐅᓗᕿᓈᕈᑎᒥᓂᓴᓇᖅᑲᑦᑕᓚᐅᕋᒃᑯ. ᑭᓯᐊᓂᓕ ᓴᓇᖑᐊᕐᓂᖅ ᖁᕕᐊᒋᓂᕐᓴᓇᓕᖅᑕᕋ, ᐊᒻᒪᓗ ᐊᖏᕋᕈᒪ ᑲᔪᓰᓐᓇᕈᒪᔪᖓ ᓴᓇᖑᐊᖃᑦᑕᕐᓗᖓ ᐅᑯᓯᓴᒥᒃ. ᐃᓚᖏᑦ ᐅᑯᓯᓴᐃᑦ ᐊᒥᐊᖏᑦ ᐊᕋᒦᖕᒋᑐᒪᑕ ᓄᓇᑎᓐᓂ: ᐱᐅᔪᑎᐋᓗᓪᓗᑎᒃ ᐅᑯᓯᓴᐃᑦ: ᖁᐱᓴᕈᐊᑦ, ᑐᖑᔪᕈᔪᖅᑐᑦ ᕿᓐᓂᖅᑕᐃᑦ ᐊᒻᒪᓗ ᑐᖑᔪᕈᔪᑐᐃᑦ ᕿᓐᓂᖅᑕᒥᒃ ᖁᐱᓴᕈᐊᓪᓛᔪᑦ.

ALEC SALA

I was born 1966 in Sanikiluaq, Nunavut. I was eight when I made my first carving of a very small seal. I lived on the Quebec side until I was 12, and then I got a job and moved back to my birthplace Sanikiluaq. In Sanikiluaq I can remember there being many carvers who mostly made carvings and sold them to support themselves. My brother and I learned to carve at the same time while we were in Sanikiluaq. When I arrived in Fenbrook I was not into carving that much and I didn't start carving right away. Finally I began to carve again and then my carvings started to improve. My favorite thing to carve is soapstone. I have tried to carve ivory but I like soapstone better. When I begin a piece, I decide what I am going to carve by looking at the soapstone. I decide by the shape of the stone. I use my memory of the animals that I have seen on the land. I never used to have the patience to finish a carving, but now I have learned to take my time. Back home I was a mostly a hunter, and carving was a way for me to pass time. Now I enjoy carving, and I look forward to carving the soapstone that I can get back home. There are some nice colours of soapstone back home: stripe, green and black, and green with black stripes.

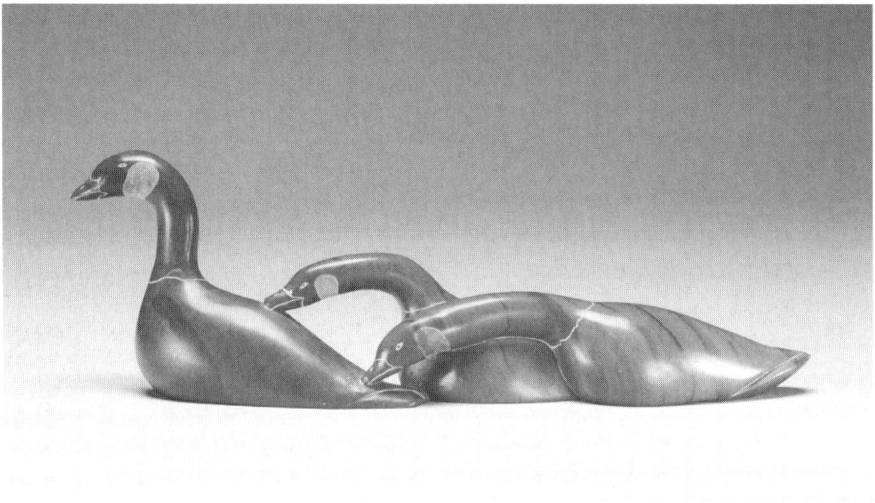

Three swimming Geese, grey soapstone, 10"- 25.4 cm

ᐱᖓᓱᑦ ᐳᐃᔾᔪᕐᑐᑦ ᓂᕐᓛᑦ, ᐃᓱᐊᖓᔪᖅ ᐅᒃᑯᓯᒃᓴᖅ

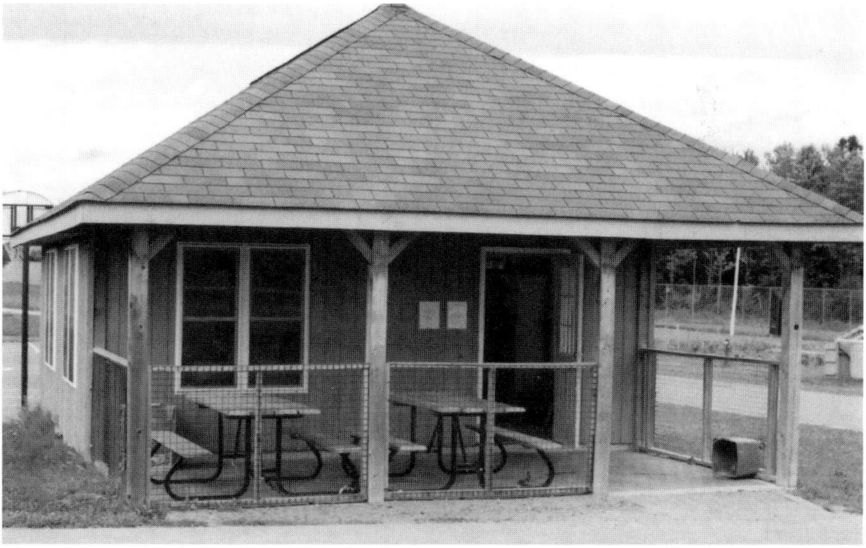

Carving shed

ᓴᓇᖕᒍᐊᕐᕕᒃ

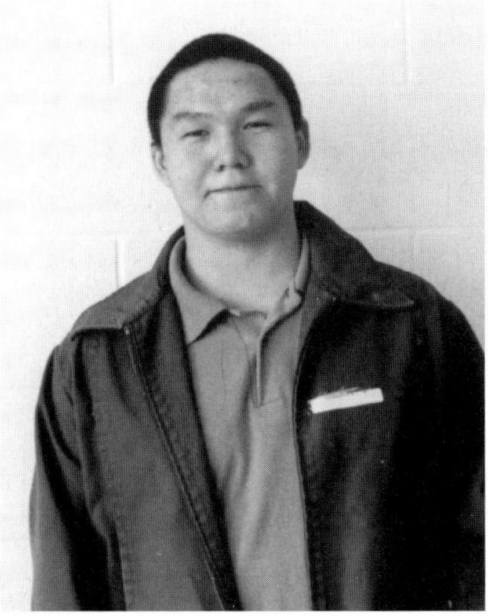

ᕈᕙᓐ ᓴᖕᑐᔭᖅ

ᐃᓄᓚᐅᓯᒪᔪᖓ ᒥᑦᑎᒪᑕᓕᒻᒥ ᓄᓇᕘᒥ, 1982-ᖑᑎᓪᓗᒍ ᓴᓇᖑᐊᖅᑲᑕᓂᓚᐅᕐᑐᖓ ᑎᒍᔭᐅᓯᒪᕕᒻᒧᖁᒪ ᐄᑉᐳᕈᒥ 2002. ᓯᕗᓪᓕᖅᐹᒥ ᓴᓇᖑᐊᔪᔭᖁ ᒪᕐᕉᒃ ᓇᑎᖑᐊᒃ. ᓯᕗᓪᓕᕐᐹᒥ ᓴᓇᖑᐊᑐᖓ ᐱᒐᓇᓚᐅᓯᒪᔪᖅ, ᑭᓯᐊᓂ ᐃᑲᔪᕐᑕᐅᔪᒪᕙᑦᑐᖓ ᐱᒐᓇᖏᓂᕐᓴᐅᔪᔪᖅ. ᐱᒋᐅᓴᐸᓕᐊᖏᓐᓇᕐᓗᓂ ᑭᓯᐊᓂ ᑕᐃᒫᒃ ᐱᒃᑲᕈᓐᓇᖕᒐᑦ. ᓴᓇᖑᐊᑲᐅᔪᒪᐃᓐᓇᕐᓯᒪᔪᖓ, ᐱᓗᐊᖅᑐᒥᒃ ᑕᑯᓐᓇᓕᖁᐃᒐᒃᑭᑦ ᓴᓇᖑᐊᕐᑏᑦ ᓴᓇᖑᐊᑎᓪᓗᒋᑦ. ᓯᕗᓪᓕᕐᐹᒥ ᐅᑯᓯᓴᒥᒃ ᓴᓇᖑᐊᑐᖓ ᐊᑐᓇᐊᖅᑲᖅᑲᑕᔪᒐᒪ ᓴᓇᖑᐊᕈᑎᓂᒃ ᑐᕚᓇᓪᓗᒍᓗ ᓴᓇᖑᐊᕐᕕᒃ ᐃᓪᓗᖁᓖᖅ. ᓯᕗᓪᓕᕐᐹᒥ ᐱᒡᒐᕈᓯᔪᔪᖓ, ᑭᓯᐊᓂ ᐃᑲᔪᕐᑕᐅᕙᑦᑐᖓ ᓴᓇᖑᐊᕐᑎᓄᑦ. ᐃᓕᑎᑕᐅᓗᖕᒐᓗ ᖃᓄᖅ ᐱᒋᐊᓇᐊᖅᑲᒻᒪᖕᒐᖅ, ᑭᓯᓕᒫᑦ ᐊᑐᓇᐊᓕᒃᑲ ᐊᑐᐃᓐᓇᕈᑦᑐᒥᑦ. ᐅᓪᓗᒥᒧᑦ ᑎᑭᑦᑐᒍ ᐊᓕᐊᓇᐅᒥᓪᓚᓇᓕᖅᑕᖁ ᐃᓕᐹᓕᖅᓯᒪᓕᖁᒪ ᓴᓇᖑᐊᑎᓂᒃ. ᑲᔪᓰᓇᕈᒪᓕᕐᑐᖓᓗ ᓴᓇᖑᐊᓂᕐᒥᒃ ᑕᐅᕗᖕᒐᓕᒫᖅ, ᑕᕝᕙᖕᒐᑦ ᑎᒍᔭᐅᓯᒪᕕᒻᒥᒃ ᐊᐅᓪᓚᕈᒪ ᑲᔪᓯᓐᓇᓚᕈᒪᔪᖓ. ᐊᒻᒪᓗ ᐃᓕᓐᓂᐊᑎᑎᖅᑲᑦᑕᕈᒪᔪᖓ ᓴᓇᖑᐊᓄᐅᓴᕈᒪᔪᓂᒃ ᓄᓇᑎᓐᓂ. ᓴᓇᖑᐊᖅᑲᑦᑕᓕᖁᒪ ᑐᑭᓯᕙᓕᕐᓯᒪᓕᕐᑐᖓ ᐱᕕᖅᑲᑎᑎᓯᒪᒪᓪᓗ ᐅᕙᓐᓂᒃ

REUBEN SANGOYA

I was born in the community of Pond Inlet, Nunavut, in 1982. I started carving in Fenbrook Institution when I arrived in April 2002. I joined the carving program because I was interested in carving and joining the program was my opportunity to learn how to carve. For my first carving I carved two seals. It was hard at first, but when I asked for help it wasn't that hard. My first carving experience was very complicated, then other guys in the program helped. They supported me by telling me not to give up and gave me advice on what kind of tools to use for certain shaping techniques. My goal is to increase my skills and to be creative at what I think is considered good carving. Being a creative carver is very important to me. I would feel this way when I would watch the skilled carvers shaping the stone. When I first tried to carve soapstone I had to borrow carving tools and I depended on the Raven carving shed tools. I was having some difficulty at first, but I asked for help and directions from the master carvers. I always thought that carving was interesting even before I came to Fenbrook and I think that I was too busy to really consider and experiment with carving until after I tried it out.

Carving at Fenbrook has been a good experience. The other carvers taught me how to begin the carving, and I became very well organized and ready to develop a soapstone carving. Whenever I needed help I would ask Lucien Tootoo most of the time, since he had told me that he was willing to help and that he had been carving for 40 to 50 years. He helped me to learn how to start and to complete a carving and gave me the good advice to rely on my own brain for creativity. To this day, I really enjoy doing a carving with the skills I have gained from a master carver. I'm hoping to continue this career of being a carver, once I leave this Institution. I also want to be able to retire from soapstone carving, and to teach other potential future carvers from my hometown. Being a new carver has given me the opportunity to

ᖃᓄᖅ ᐃᓄᐃᑦ ᐱᖅᑯᓯᙵᑎᑐᑦ ᓴᓇᙳᐊᓂᕐᒥᒃ. ᐃᓕᓴᕆᔭᐅᓚᕈᒪᔪᙵ ᓯᓚᔪᐊᒥᐅᓄᑦ ᓴᓇᙳᐊᑎᐅᓂᖓᓄᑦ. ᑭᓇᐅᔭᓂᒃ ᓄᐊᓴᐃᑲᓯᐊᕐᑏᑦ ᐊᑭᑦᑐᕋᐅᑎᑎᑎᓪᓗᒋᑦ ᐅᕙᓐᓂᒃ ᐱᕕᖅᑲᑎᑎᓯᒪᒍᑦ ᑐᓂᓯᓂᕐᒥᒃ ᓄᓇᕗᒧᑦ ᐅᕙᙵ ᓄᓇᙵᓄᑦ, ᐊᒻᒪᓗ ᐅᐱᒋᔾᔪᑎᒋᓪᓗᒍ. ᖁᕕᐊᓱᑦᑐᙵ ᐃᓕᐹᓕᕐᓯᒪᙵ ᓴᓇᙳᐊᓂᕐᒥᒃ ᑎᒍᔭᐅᓯᒪᕕᒻᒥᑐᙵ. ᖁᕕᐊᒋᓪᓗᒍᓗ ᐅᑯᓯᓴᓂᒃ ᓴᓇᙳᐊᕆᐊᓴ. ᓯᕗᓂᑎᓐᓂ ᐊᔨᒋᙵᒋᑦᑐᓂᒃ ᐆᑐᖅᑲᑦᕈᒪᒥᔪᙵ ᐆᑦᑐᑎᒋᓪᓗᒍ ᓇᔾᔪᒥᓂᕐᓂᒃ.

fully understand the true meaning of a carver with traditional knowledge and skills. I hope to be recognized by the world as a good soapstone carver. Being a part of the Inside Out Charity Auction has given me the opportunity to contribute to the Nunavut Territory that I lived in, and I am proud of that. I am happy that I have learned to carve at Fenbrook. I like to carve soapstone. I would like to try other carving media in the future, like antler. I think that teaching others how to carve is culturally important only if they are interested, or want to know about carving cultural things. I would teach my child and future children to carve and encourage them to learn about our culture. My carvings tell a story depending on what the shape of the stone is, while other carvings are cultural symbols. In the future I would like to carve human figures and shamans.

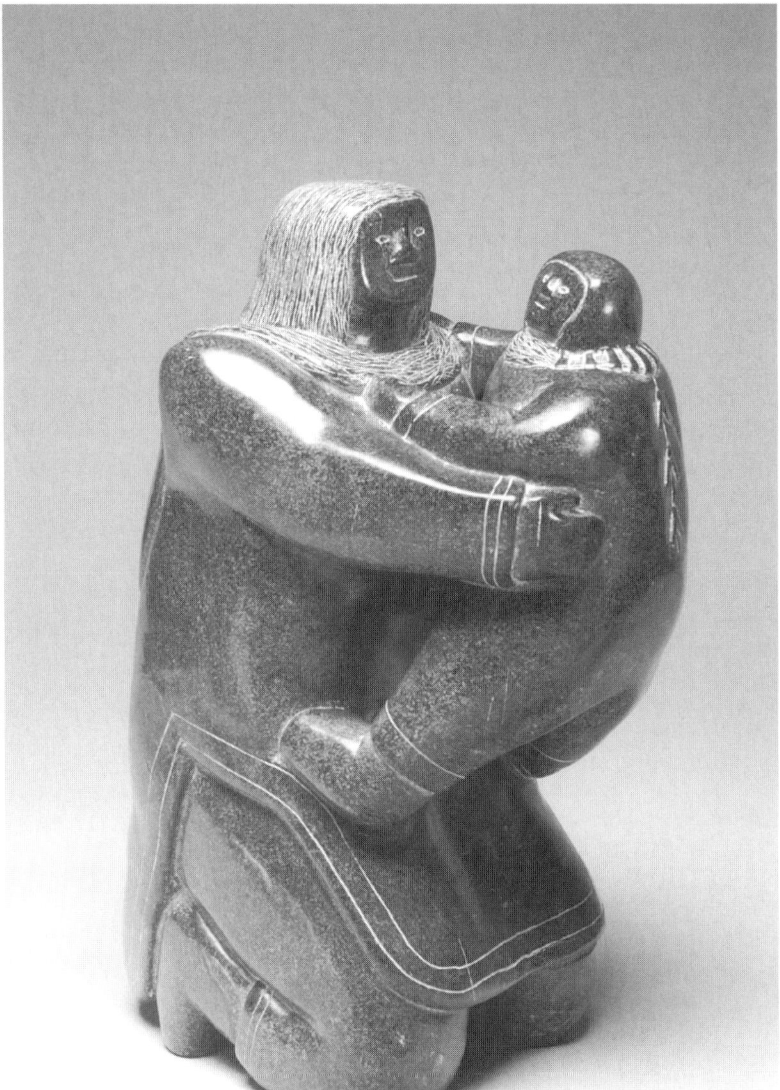

Kneeling Inuit mother holding her child, mottled grey soapstone, 13"- 33 cm

ᓯᕐᑯᖓᓗᓂ ᐃᓄᒃ ᐋᓇᓇᐅᔪᖅ ᕿᑐᖓᒥᓂᒃ ᑎᑰᒥᐊᑐᖅ, ᐃᓱᐊᖓᔪᖅ ᐅᒃᑯᓯᔅᓴᖅ

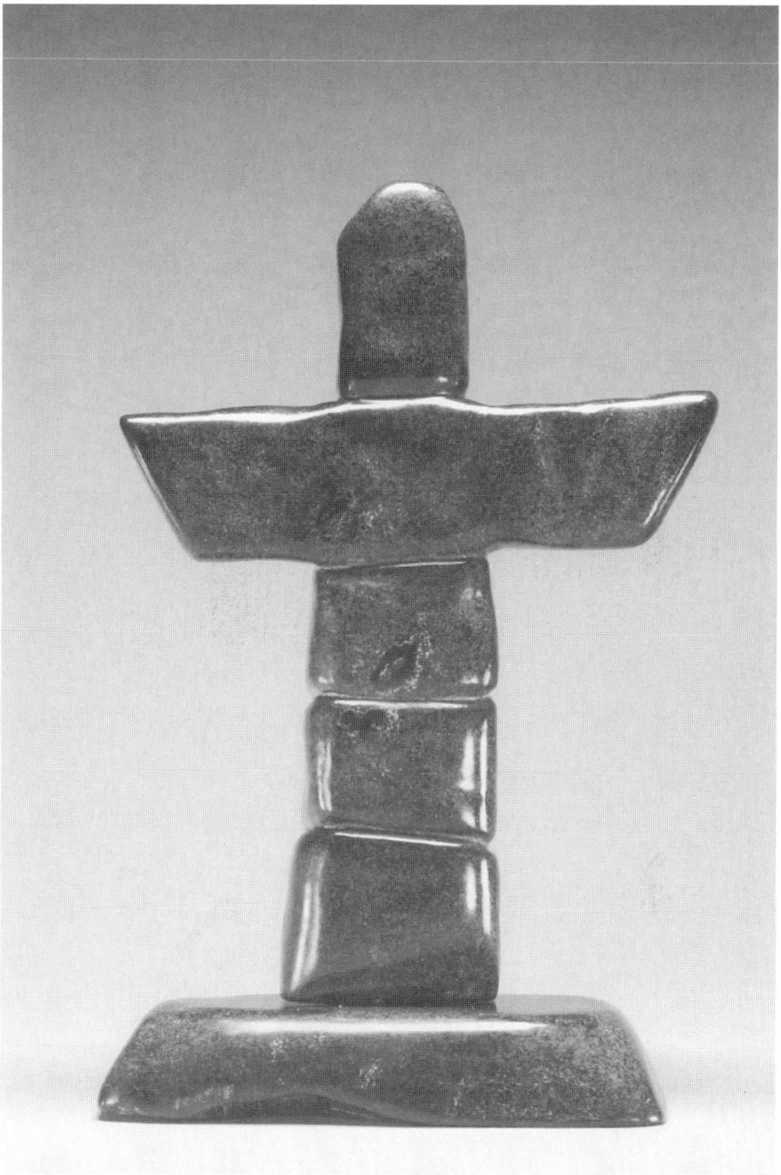

Inukshuk, mottled dark soapstone, 11"- 27.9 cm

ᐃᓄᒃᓱᒃ, ᕿᓐᓈᖕᒪᔪᖅ ᐅᒃᑯᓯᔅᓴᖅ

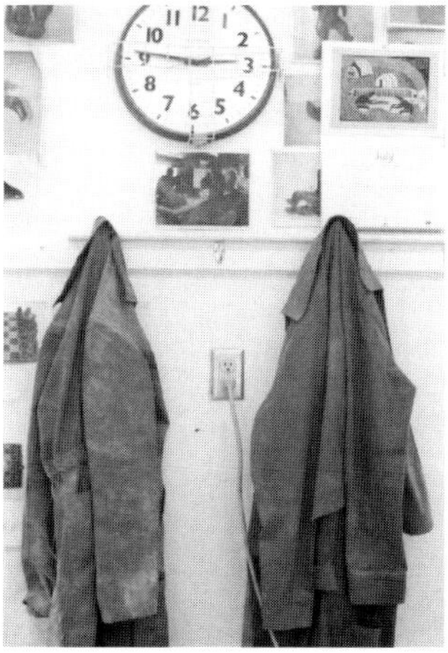

ᑕᑯᓐᓇᕐᓂᖅ ᓱᕗᓂᕐᒧᑦ

ᐊᕐᕌᒍᑦ 50-ᐅᓗᐊᓕᖅᑐᑦ, ᐃᓄᐃᑦ ᓴᓇᙳᐊᒐᙱᑦ ᐊᓯᔾᔨᐸᓪᓕᐊᓂᖅᑲᒻᒪᓇᔅᓯᒪᕗᑦ. ᓲᕐᓗ ᓴᓇᙳᐊᓯᒪᓂᙱᑦ, ᖁᓪᓚᐸᓪᓖᖅᑐᑎᓪᓗ, ᑭᓱᑐᐃᓐᓇᐃᑦ ᐊᓯᔾᔨᓯᒪᒻᒪᓇᑉᐳᑦ ᐃᓄᐃᓪᓗ ᐊᙳᓇᓱᖅᑦᑕᓚᐅᕐᑑᒐᓗᐊᑦ ᐊᙳᓇᓱᓐᓂᕐᒥᒃ ᐱᒻᒪᕆᖅᑲᙱᓂᖅᓴᐅᓕᕐᑐᑎᒃ ᖃᓪᓗᓈ ᐱᖅᑯᓯᙱᑎᑐᑦ ᐄᓄᓂᖅᓴᐅᓕᕐᑐᑎᒃ, ᓄᓇᑖᕐᑐᑎᓪᓗ ᓇᒻᒥᓂᖅ.

ᑕᐃᔅᓱᒪᓂ ᐃᓄᐃᑦ ᓴᓇᙳᐊᖅᑦᑕᐸᓪᓕᐊᓕᕐᑎᓪᓗᒋᑦ ᐱᑕᖅᑲᓗᐊᓚᐅᙱᓚᖅ ᓴᓇᙳᐊᕋᔅᓴᒥᒃ ᐊᔾᕐᓇᓂᖅᓴᐅᖅᑦᑕᓚᐅᙱᓪᓗ ᐄᓄᒐᓱᐊᕐᓂᒃᑯᑦ. ᓴᓇᙳᐊᕋᔅᓴᐃᓪᓗ ᒥᑭᔫᑎᐅᓪᓗᑎᒃ, ᓴᓇᙳᐊᕐᐸᓚᐅᕐᑯᑦ ᓴᐅᓂᕐᓂᒃ, ᐅᖏᓘᓐᓃᑦ ᑑᒫᓂᒃ ᐊᒻᒪᓗ ᓇᔾᔪᒦᓂᑦ ᑐᑦᑐᒧᑦ. ᓴᓇᓯᒪᑎᐊᙱᓐᓂᓴᐅᖅᑦᑕᓚᐅᕐᑐᑦ ᓲᕐᓗ ᐋᖅᑭᓯᒪᓂᙱᑦ ᐊᑖᙱᙱᓂᖅᓴᐅᓪᓗᑎᒃ ᐊᓐᓅᖕᒍᐊᓕᐅᓯᒪᓂᖅᓴᐅᓪᓗᑎᒃ ᐊᒻᒪᓗ ᓱᓇᑯᑕᒃᑲᙳᐊᙳᓂᖅᓴᐅᓪᓗᑎᒃ. ᑕᒪᓐᓇ ᐊᓯᔾᔨᐸᓪᓕᐊᓕᓚᐅᖅᑐᖅ ᐃᓄᐃᑦ ᓄᓇᓕᓐᓄᑦ ᓅᑉᐸᓪᓕᐊᓕᕐᑎᓪᓗᒋᑦ 1950 ᐊᑯᓐᓂᙵᓂ. ᐃᓄᐃᑦ ᓄᓇᓕᓐᓂ ᓄᓇᖃᓕᕐᑎᓪᓗᒋ ᓴᓇᙳᐊᒐᙱᑦ ᓴᖅᑭᐸᓪᓕᐊᒋᐊᓯᓚᐅᖅᑯᑦ. ᐊᖕᒋᔫᑕᐅᓂᖅᓴᐅᓕᕐᑐᑎᓪᓗ ᓴᓇᙳᐊᕋᓴᐃᑦ ᐱᑕᖅᑲᓐᓂᓴᐅᓕᓚᐅᖅᑯᑦ, ᓂᐅᕕᐊᙳᒍᒪᓂᖅᓴᐅᓕᖅᑐᑎᓪᓗ, ᓴᓇᙳᐊᓲᑦ ᓄᓇᐅᑉ ᐊᓯᐊᓄᑦ ᓄᑦᑎᕋᔾᔪᙱᓂᓴᐅᓕᓚᐅᖕᒐᑕ ᐊᖕᒋᓂᖅᓴᓂᓪᓗ ᓴᓇᙳᕋᔅᓴᒃᑲᓕᕐᑐᑎᒃ.

ᐊᓯᔾᔨᖅᓯᒪᓂᖅᓴᐅᓕᕐᑐᖅ ᓴᓇᙳᐊᕐᓂᐅᑉᐳᖅ ᒫᓐᓇᐅᔪᖅ, ᓲᕐᓗ ᐱᖅᑕᐅᓗᑎᒃ ᑎᑎᕐᑐᒐᐃᑦ, ᒪᕋᐃᑦ ᐊᒻᒪᓗ ᓴᕕᕋᔾᔭᐃᑦ. ᓴᓇᙳᐊᑎᐅᔪᑦ ᐱᖅᑯᓯᒥᓂᒃ ᓴᖅᑭᑎᑎᑉᐸᓪᓕᐊᓕᓚᐅᖅᑯᑦ ᓴᓇᙳᐊᒐᒃᑯᑦ. ᓅᑕᕈᐸᓪᓕᐊᓗᑎᓪᓗ ᑭᓱᑐᐃᓐᓇᐃᑦ, ᐅᐊᔭᒨᕐᑐᒧᓪᓗ ᓴᓇᙳᐊᕈᑎᑦᑲᓕᕐᑐᓂ, ᓴᓇᙳᐊᑏᑦ ᐱᕕᔅᓴᖃᓐᓂᖅᓴᐅᓕᖅᑯᑦ ᐱᔭᕆᐊᑭᓐᓂᓴᐅᓕᖅᑯᓪᓗ ᒫᓐᓇᐅᔪᖅ. ᐅᑭᐅᕐᑕᕐᑐᒥᐅᑦ ᓴᓇᙳᐊᕐᑏᑦ ᖃᐅᔨᑎᑎᓯᓕᐊᓂᓴᐅᓕᖅᑯᑦ ᓴᓇᙳᐊᒐᒥᒍᑦ. ᐃᓕᓴᕆᔭᐅᓯᓪᓕᐊᓗᑎᓪᓗ ᓯᓚᕐᔪᐊᕐᒥᐅᓄᑦ. ᐊᑭᖕᒐᓗ ᖁᑉᐸᓕᕐᓯᒪᓂᖅᓴᐅᓕᖅᑯᖅ ᒫᓐᓇᐅᔪᖅ, ᓴᓇᙳᐊᖅᑦᑕᓂᖅᓴᐅᓕᖅᑯᓪᓗ ᖃᐅᔨᓯᒪᓕᕋᒥᒃ ᑮᓇᐅᔭᓕᐅᕈᑎᑎᐊᑉᐅᓂᙵᓂᒃ ᐃᓚᒌᓄᑦ.

ᐃᓄᐃᑦ ᓴᓇᙳᐊᒐᙱᑦ ᒫᓐᓇᐅᔪᖅ ᐱᕈᕐᐸᓕᐊᖕᒋᓐᓇᓕᖅᑯᑦ ᑲᔪᓯᑉᐸᓕᐊᖕᒋᓐᓇᓕᕐᑐᑎᓪᓗ. ᓱᑲᐃᑐᒥᒃ, ᐊᑉᕕᐊᕈᑏᑦ ᐊᓂᒍᐸᓪᓕᐊᓯᒪᕗᑦ ᓲᕐᓗ ᐅᖅᑲᖅᑎᒦᓐᓂᒃᑯᑦ ᐅᖕᒐᓯᖕᒋᖕᒋᓂᖅᓴᐅᓕᕐᑐᑎᒃ, ᐃᓚᖕᒋᓪᓗ ᓴᓇᙳᐊᑏᑦ ᖃᓪᓗᓈᑦ ᓄᓇᖕᒐᓐᓂ ᓄᓇᑖᕐᐸᓕᐊᓪᓗᑎᒃ; ᐊᑯᓂᐅᖕᒋᑐᓪᓗᓃᑦ ᐃᓚᖕᒋᑦ ᓄᓇᖅᑲᑲᐃᓐᓇᐸᑦᑐᑎᒃ; ᐃᓄᐃᑦ

LOOKING TO THE FUTURE

Over the last fifty years, contemporary Canadian Inuit art has undergone a breathtaking evolution. Style, scale, subject matter and materials have changed significantly as the artists themselves have gone from a migratory hunting lifestyle to townspeople living in the modern, self-governing territory of Nunavut.

The creation of works of art in traditional culture was limited by the scarcity of available materials and the realities of a harsh lifestyle. Sculptures were tiny, primarily made of bone, ivory and antler. Graphic expression was limited to the decoration of tools and clothing. This changed greatly as the Inuit began to move into settlements after 1950. With this transition to permanent residence, sculptures of greater scale and complexity could be conceived for the first time. Larger pieces of stone became available with new quarrying methods, and artists who were no longer migratory were able to work in larger scale.

New means of artistic expression were introduced, including prints, textiles, ceramics and metalwork. These allowed artists to diversify their traditional graphic and sculptural artistic expression. New technologies, including power tools, allowed the artists to achieve greater complexity in their compositions. At the same time, as artists in the north were embracing these new possibilities for their art, a strong national and international market for Inuit art was developing in the south. The market developed and, for the first time, making art could be viewed as a means of providing for the family – so more time could be devoted to it.

Contemporary Inuit art continues to evolve and develop. Slowly, the twin barriers of distance and communication are being surmounted. Some artists have chosen to live in the south, either temporarily or permanently. The younger generations are primarily bilingual; easier travel to the south and increased telecommunications mean that the artist is more readily able to represent himself to his audience in the south.

ᓄᑲᑎᐅᓂᓴᐃᑦ ᒫᓐᓇᐅᓕᕐᑐᖅ ᒪᕐᕉᓐᓂᒃ ᐅᕐᑲᐅᓰᓐᓂᒃ ᐅᕐᑲᕈᓐᓇᓯᓪᓗᑎᑉ; ᐊᔪᕐᓇᖕᒋᓐᓂᓴᐅᓕᕐᑐᓂᓗ ᓇᓕᐊᓐᓄᕋᓇᐊᓴᖅ ᐊᐅᓚᕐᑲᑦᑕᓂᒃᑯᑦ ᕐᑲᓪᓗᓈᑦ ᓄᓇᖕᒐᓐᓄᑦ. ᑐᓴᐅᒪᕐᑲᑕᐅᑎᒍᓐᓇᓂᓴᐅᓕᕐᑐᑎᓪᓗ ᓴᓇᖕᒍᐊᑏᑦ. ᕐᑲᐅᔨᒪᔭᐅᑎᐸᓪᓕᐊᖕᒋᓇᖅᑯᑦ ᑕᑯᔭᐅᑎᑉᐸᓕᐊᓪᓗᑎᓪᓗ ᓇᒻᒥᓂᖅ ᕐᑲᓪᓗᓈᑦ ᓄᓇᖕᒐᓂᒥᐅᓄᑦ

ᐊᑲᐅᖕᒋᓕᐅᕈᑕᐅᕙᑦᑐᑦ ᐊᑦᑐᐃᓂᕐᑲᒻᒪᓇᔅᓯᒪᕗᑦ ᐃᓄᓐᓂᒃ ᑭᓯᐊᓂ ᓴᓇᖕᒍᐊᕐᑲᑦᑕᕐᓂᖅ ᑲᔪᓰᓇᖅᓯᒪᕗᖅ ᐅᑭᐅᑕᕐᑐᒥ. ᐃᓄᐃᓪᓗ ᐱᕐᑯᓯᖕᒐ ᑕᑯᓴᐅᑎᑕᐅᖕᒋᓇᖅᑐᓂ ᓴᓇᖕᒍᐊᒐᒃᑯᑦ. ᐊᒥᓱᑦ ᕐᑲᓪᓗᓈᓂᒥᐅᑦ ᑐᑭᓯᐅᒪᓚᐅᖅᑯᑦ ᓴᓇᖕᒍᐊᒐᖕᒋᑦ ᐃᓄᐃᑦ ᐊᓯᔾᔨᓛᕐᓂᖕᒋᓐᓂᒃ 1950 ᐱᒋᐊᐸᓪᓕᐊᓕᕐᑎᓪᓗᒍ, ᑕᒪᐅᓇ ᕐᑲᐃᔨᑎᑦᑏᕙᓪᓕᕐᓯᒪᕗᑦ ᐃᓄᐃᑦ ᓴᓇᖕᒍᐊᖕᒐᖕᒋᑎᒍᑦ ᑲᑎᑎᑦᑏᕙᓕᑐᑎᓪᓗ ᑭᒃᑯᑐᐃᓐᓇᕐᓂᒃ ᑐᑭᓯᔭᐅᕚᓪᓕᑎᑎᓪᓗᑎᑉ ᐃᓄᐃᑦ ᐊᔨᒋᔭᐅᓐᓂᖕᒋᓐᓂ ᓲᕐᓗ ᐱᖅᑯᓯᒥᒍᑦ, ᕐᑯᕕᐊᒋᔭᐅᖕᒋᓐᓇᖅᑯᑦ ᐅᓪᓗᒥᐅᔪᖅ ᑲᓇᑕᒥᐅᓄᑦ.

ᓯᓚ ᒫᓐᓇᐅᔪᖅ ᓴᓇᖕᒍᐊᒐᐃᑦ ᐅᓂᒃᑲᐅᓯᐅᓂᖕᒐ ᕐᑲᐅᔨᓴᐅᕙᓪᓚᐊᑐᐃᓐᓇᖅᑯᑦ. ᓴᓇᖕᒍᐊᑎᓪᓚᓈᑦ ᐃᓚᓴᓇᔭᐅᕙᓪᓚᐊᑐᐃᓐᓇᖅᑯᑦ ᑎᓕᐅᖅᑕᐅᒥᐊᓪᓚᑐᑎᓪᓗ. ᐱᒋᐅᑉᐸᓪᓚᐊᑐᐃᓐᓇᖅᑯᑦ ᐃᓚᓴᓇᔭᐅᑎᑎᐸᓪᓚᐊᓗᑎᓪᓗ. ᑐᑭᓯᔭᐅᕙᓪᓚᐊᑎᑦᑏᓇᖅᑯᑦ ᓴᓇᖕᒍᐊᒐᒃᑯᑦ ᐃᓄᐃᑦ ᕐᑲᓄᖅ ᐃᓱᒫᓗᑎᒋᕙᑦᑕᖕᒋᓐᓂᒃ ᐅᕝᕙᓗ ᕐᑲᓄᐃᑐᓂᖕᒋᓐᓂᒃ. ᐊᒻᒪᓗ ᑕᑯᓐᓇᖕᒍᐊᕋᓴᓂᑎᑎᓂᓴᐅᓪᓗᑎᑉ ᐃᓄᐃᑦ ᓄᓇᖕᒐᑦ ᐅᑭᐅᖕᒍᐃᓇᖕᒋᒻᒪᑦ, ᓱᕐᑯᐃᓯᑎᑏᕙᓕᓯᒪᓗᑎᑦ ᐅᓪᓗᒥᐅᔪᖅ ᓴᖕᒋᔪᐋᓗᒻᒪᑕ ᐱᖅᑯᓯᕐᒥᒍᑦ.

Social changes in the north have certainly had an effect, and yet Inuit artists continue to portray the traditional culture through their work. Many in the south predicted, as early as the 1950's, that Inuit carvings would lose their distinctive qualities and fall prey to commercialization. Instead, contemporary Inuit artists have melded tradition with innovation in their works of art which are among the most exciting and dynamic in Canada today.

The story of contemporary Inuit art is still unfolding. The developments of the last half-century have allowed truly talented artists the opportunity to be recognized and encouraged. The individual growth and formal concerns of these artists are the key to the ongoing successful evolution of Inuit art. No longer a reflection of a past life in the frozen north, it speaks of today's reality, filtered through a still vibrant culture.

Patricia Feheley
Feheley Fine Arts, Toronto

ACKNOWLEDGEMENTS

The publisher would like to thank the carvers, Correctional Service Canada – Ontario Region, Allan Briesmaster, Evan Heise, Janice Marin, Sylvia Purdon, Mike Provan, Patricia Feheley, Myna Ishulutak, Waddington's Auctioneers and Appraisers, and Leetia Kowalchuk, who made this book possible.